Human Rights Interventions

Series Editors
Chiseche Mibenge, Stanford University, Stanford, CA, USA
Irene Hadiprayitno, Leiden University, Leiden, Zuid-Holland, The Netherlands

The traditional human rights frame creates a paradigm by which the duty bearer's (state) and rights holder's (civil society organizations) interests collide over the limits of enjoyment and enforcement. The series departs from the paradigm by centering peripheral yet powerful actors that agitate for intervention and influence in the (re)shaping of rights discourse in the midst of grave insecurities. The series privileges a call and response between theoretical inquiry and empirical investigation as contributors critically assess human rights interventions mediated by spatial, temporal, geopolitical and other dimensions. An interdisciplinary dialogue is key as the editors encourage multiple approaches such as law and society, political economy, historiography, legal ethnography, feminist security studies, and multi-media.

More information about this series at
https://link.springer.com/bookseries/15595

Damien Rogers

Wars, Laws, Rights and the Making of Global Insecurities

palgrave
macmillan

Damien Rogers
Auckland, New Zealand

Human Rights Interventions
ISBN 978-3-030-90161-5 ISBN 978-3-030-90162-2 (eBook)
https://doi.org/10.1007/978-3-030-90162-2

This Palgrave Macmillan imprint is published by the registered company Springer Nature Switzerland AG
The registered company address is: Gewerbestrasse 11, 6330 Cham, Switzerland

Acknowledgments

First and foremost, I wish to acknowledge Massey University's College of Humanities and Social Sciences, New Zealand, for sustaining me—intellectually, materially and financially—for much of the past decade. I wish to acknowledge here, too, my Head of School, Professor Glenn Banks, for easing the load when that load was too heavy for my shoulders to bear.

I want to thank my colleagues who have shown interest in my research and mention two on the Albany Campus in Auckland who stand out to me as outstanding human beings: Grant Duncan and Nick Nelson. I value their friendship, wise counsel and even temperaments in the face of my ever-present irascible and unreasonable tendencies. I also want to thank my editor at Palgrave Macmillan, Dr. Anca Pusca, for her encouragement and ongoing support.

I am very grateful to Springer Nature for granting me permission to reuse material (first published online) from chapters I have written for *Human Rights in War*, a volume I had the privilege of editing as part of the Major Reference Works in the series on International Human Rights. The chapters I draw on here are:

Rogers D. (2021). Concepts of War and International Human Rights. In: Rogers D. (ed.) *Human Rights in War*. International Human Rights. Springer, Singapore. https://doi.org/10.1007/978-981-15-5202-1_2-1.

Rogers D. (2021). Laws of Political Violence. In: Rogers D. (ed.) *Human Rights in War*. International Human Rights. Springer, Singapore. https://doi.org/10.1007/978-981-15-5202-1_7-1.
Rogers D. (2021). *Anthropolemos*. In: Rogers D. (ed) *Human Rights in War*. International Human Rights. Springer, Singapore. https://doi.org/10.1007/978-981-15-5202-1_18-1.
Rogers D. (2021). An Evolving Research Agenda for International Human Rights in War. In: Rogers D. (ed.) *Human Rights in War*. International Human Rights. Springer, Singapore. https://doi.org/10.1007/978-981-15-5202-1_19-1.

Material taken from these chapters has been reconfigured, revised and reworked here into what I hope is a focused and coherent argument about the making of global insecurities and the enormous stakes that are involved.

My gratitude extends to the two anonymous reviewers who provided their constructive and informed advice on the book's proposal and draft manuscript. Dr. John Battersby, Dr. Lucas Knotter and Associate Professor Grant Duncan also provided me with useful feedback on earlier versions of the chapters comprising this book. The book is undoubtedly stronger as a result of this expert and erudite input, though any errors and all misdemeanors, intellectual or otherwise, are mine and mine alone.

Last, but certainly not least, my family, close friends and partner, Sarah, deserve a thousand and one accolades each for being there for me as I journeyed, once again, through a long dark night into the dawning brightness of day. Sadly, I lost another dear friend along the way; and it is to your memory, Dr. Carl Bradley, that I dedicate this book. As you depart from this life and make your way toward whatever lies next for us in the beyond, I hope the thirst is upon you my friend—Sláinte!

Contents

CHAPTER 1

Introduction

Abstract This opening chapter explains what it means to undertake a political analysis of global insecurity which foregrounds the ways in which these insecurities are produced and sustained through struggles over war, international law, and human rights. It suggests that this kind of political analysis is a very serious matter because these global insecurities may well result in the end of almost all life on our planet and, as such, ought to prompt some deep reflection on what it means to be human. This chapter situates this political analysis within the politico-cultural project of modernity and its penchant for a reason before introducing the concepts found in the work of Michel Foucault, Pierre Bourdieu, and Bruno Latour, which help make sense of these insecurities. It closes by signalling the organisation of the book's central argument.

Keywords Politics · Analysis · Modernity · Anthropocentricism · Humanity

This short book explores the very large, complex and vexing issues of war, international law and human rights, as well as some of the interconnections among them. It examines war as a foundational problem for analysts of contemporary world affairs, and as an enduring and unruly type of

D. Rogers, *Wars, Laws, Rights and the Making of Global Insecurities*, Human Rights Interventions,
https://doi.org/10.1007/978-3-030-90162-2_1

political violence posing challenges to those seeking to govern these world affairs while presenting them with opportunities to demonstrate the value of their roles and responsibilities. It considers international law as a major response to war, among other types of political violence, and as an antidote to the harms accompanying that violence, which can also serve to entrench the hierarchies found in the international status quo. Human rights receive attention here, too, because the promotion and protection of these rights feature often as the proclaimed purpose behind collective efforts to surpass the rule of tooth and claw. In what follows, I cast light on how the politics of war, law and rights produce serious global insecurities in large part because of an anthropocentric commitment that lies at the heart of the modernist project, which underlies and animates the struggles among individuals and groups to govern these world affairs for their respective ends, places humanity in grave danger by imperiling other life forms and life systems on this planet. This anthropocentric commitment also produces and sustains ontological myopia that enacts limits to our collective understanding of the scale and depth of these global insecurities and the enormity of the stakes involved.

This book constitutes an analysis; that is, it seeks to break down a topic into its component parts and to understand the relationships among those parts to one another, as well as to understand the relationships between those parts to the whole. In this case, the topic grasped is global insecurities and its components are wars, laws and rights. The configurations of power that underscore the relationships among these parts, and between these parts and the whole, can be best described as political. I understand politics to be something broader than the contestations that occur in national assembles and parliaments throughout the world. I also understand politics to be something broader than the contestations that occur between nation-states. Indeed, I understand politics in the broadest possible sense where it refers to "all those things we do, individually and in concert, to get and use power over others for non-trivial purposes. Politics is always about trying to get our way to some substantive end. It is always a verb" (Pettman 2001: 6). This book, then, is a political analysis of serious global insecurities and the ways in which those insecurities are produced—sometimes unwittingly, at other times callously—by struggles over war, international law and human rights. These global insecurities are multitudinous rather than singular, register in varying ways and to differing extents, and are evolving and more profound than the insecurities produced by the international relations conducted by diplomats, generals and state-makers, though these actors are not disinterested parties either. These global insecurities are truly profound because they can call time on almost all life residing on this planet. These insecurities, which I believe are intractable and, thus, unlikely to dissipate any time soon, necessitate an equally profound rethinking of what it means to be human in the years to come.

This book's analysis is framed by the context, logic and practices of the politico-cultural project of modernity. By "politico-culture," I mean "'deep' politics on a global scale, since it is about human beings getting their way on planet earth. It is about a human capacity that has made us highly successful in Darwinian terms, at least, for the moment" (Pettman 2001: 42). While the term "project" implies modernity was planned, it was not and no person could have anticipated or designed everything it entails. The term, however, does signal the active and intentional construction of such a world without implying the existence of an overall proposal or grand scheme (Pettman 2001: 156).

Modernity is characterized here by its commitment to the idea that the human mind should mentally objectify everything. By using reason as a way of knowing, modernists are able to explain how the material world functions. Where they cannot explain a phenomenon, they research and analyze it until they can, though of course many unanswered questions remain as mysteries. The results of such scientific endeavors enabled modernists to increasingly have their way over others in non-trivial matters. Pettman elaborates further when he writes:

> Rationalism is not a new ideology. Nor is it particular to Europeans. Individuals in every culture and in every era have found the rationalist principle enlightening and emancipatory. Europeans were the first to make it the basis for a whole culture, however, and they have had extraordinary success in doing so, not least because of the extraordinary reliability of this way of knowing when used to analyse non-human affairs. European rationalists subsequently came to create a sharp contrast between reason's capacity to arrive at truth by itself, and the capacity to know the world via the senses and experiences. (2001: 8–9)

The sustained application of the faculty of reason enabled individuals and groups to access and share a common view of reality, to collect empirical data and observe phenomena, and to propose and test theories about the ways in which the natural world functions. This new understanding of reality and search for truth opened spaces to contest religious dogma and other received wisdoms. It provided the fertile intellectual ground for the production of new knowledge in the natural sciences, such as Charles Darwin's theory of evolution, which situated the origins of humanity alongside other life species (Pettman 2001: 284) but implied humanity's superiority over non-human life and demonstrated its unrivaled mastery of the natural world.

While many see rationality as a reaction against the authority of the church (Tarnas 1991), John Gray suggests that modernity replaces faith in religion with a faith in reason and that modern politics is a chapter in the history of religion (2007). Stephen Toulmin is especially astute when he explains:

> Despite all the ambiguities surrounding the idea of Modernity, and the varied dates that different people give for its origin, the confusions and disagreements hide an underlying consensus .... All parties to the debate agree that the self-styled "new philosophers" of the 17th century were responsible for new ways of thinking about nature in a new and "scientific" way, and to use more "rational" methods to deal with the problems of human life and society. Their work was therefore a turning point in European history, and deserves to be marked off as the true starting point of Modernity. (1990: 9–10)

This uninhibited life of the mind took hold, then, as a society-wide practice in Europe during the seventeenth century, though perhaps its most successful early proponents are found in the political experiment that gave birth to the United States of America. From there, western-styled modernity spread southwards and northwards, and the eastwards across the Pacific to Asia, and did so "in ever increasing numbers, slaughtering and enslaving, preaching and impounding. They spread their maladies. They brought new kinds of medicine. The pedaled their machine-made goods. They taught rational-legal techniques of public administration and organization. They took land" (Pettman 2001: 85). Modernity was able to spread because its central characteristic—the use of reason as an end into itself practiced *en masse*—produced technologies, including weapons and exchangeable commodities, that were superior to those found elsewhere. The material power that this way of thinking about the world enabled, and the magnificent achievements of that material power, helped those at the helm of the modernist project achieve ascendency over others.

The politico-cultural project of modernity helped give rise to internationally recognized human rights because it constitutes a set of material and ideational conditions that valorize a certain sense of self-identity ahead of others. This type of self-identity coheres around the individual or, more precisely, individualism, though there are of course alternative ways in which to articulate one's sense of self, including through embracing nationalism or participating in global social movements as collective forms of identity that aim to compensate for the feelings of alienation that modern individuals experience (Pettman 2001). Richard Tarnas usefully sums up the rise of this new individualism in the following terms:

> And so between the fifteenth and seventeenth centuries, the West saw the emergence of a newly self-conscious and autonomous human being—curious about the world, confident in his own judgements, skeptical of orthodoxies, rebellious against authority, responsible for his own belief and actions, armored of the classical past but even more committed to a greater future, proud of his humanity, conscious of his distinctiveness from nature, aware of his artistic powers as individual creator, assured of his intellectual capacity to comprehend and control nature, and altogether less dependent on an omnipotent god. (1991: 282)

Unsurprisingly, most modernists express a fierce commitment to individualism that includes proclaiming certain personal freedoms and articulating these as rights to be protected against state or societal interference (Pettman 2010). This intense and enduring commitment to individualism is not without costs, however, as a focus on humanity as a species demonstrates. Indeed, taking focus on the scale of the human species, rather than on units of analysis more commonly found in the work of legal scholars, social sciences researchers and International Relations academics—such as the sovereign state or the wider states-based system; and individuals or various forms of collective identity—draws attention to the ways in which the limits of humanity are enacted against other life forms, some of which are species that have not yet obtained rights comparable to those enjoyed by human beings even though they are also sentient beings that feel emotions and exercise intellect.

Modernity also provides the conditions which make possible the Anthropocene—a term referring to an epoch marked by humanity's pernicious impact on the planet and its life-supporting systems; in fact, the construction of the Anthropocene as a reified object, which is then considered by the rationalist mind gaze is, of course, the result of a fundamentally modernist practice that enacts the estrangement of humanity from the natural world and non-human life forms. This is not to say, however, that rationality is the prime cause of the Anthropocene, but rather, to highlight that reason is a key characteristic of the modernist project which enabled the Anthropocene's emergence. While the term Modernity is not a synonym for the term the Anthropocene, there are undoubtedly important interconnections.

I take a critical perspective on the conduct of contemporary world affairs and draw on concepts found in the work of Michel Foucault, Pierre Bourdieu and Bruno Latour to cast new light on the ways in which the politics of war, laws and rights produce serious global insecurities. While other key thinkers have profound insights to share, the work of Foucault Bourdieu and Latour continue to shape my own thinking on wars, laws and rights as they have each, in their own way, challenged conventional thinking about the modernist project, prompting me and others to reconsider the recurring problems of the human condition. Scholars have also examined the contributions of Foucault (Jabre 2007; Dillon and Neal 2008; Bonditti et al. 2017) and Bourdieu to the study of contemporary world affairs (Adler-Nissen 2013; Bigo 2011). In this respect, I concur with Andrew W. Neal when he observes that Foucault's work disrupts key concepts found in disciplinary International Relations, offers new ways of thinking through issues of power and political practice, and provides useful concepts such as problematization, discourse and genealogy (Neal 2009: 161). I similarly concur with Peter Jackson's description of Bourdieu's work as "a critique of the cultural dynamics of domination" that uses new concepts, including the field and symbolic violence, to better understand and explain how social hierarchies and power relations are preserved and sustained by various practices (Jackson 2009: 102). Scholars who consider the making of global insecurities, and the roles played by the politics of wars, laws and rights, seldom—if ever—draw on the work of these three thinkers at the same time. But I have, as I hope this book shows, found doing so immensely productive.

This book comprises three main chapters, dealing, respectively, with the politics of war, international law and human rights. In my first chapter,

I suggest the phenomenon of war is a foundational problem for analysts of contemporary world affairs, and that these analysts encounter significant empirical obstacles and conceptual difficulties when they provide accounts of war. I explain how state aggression and armed conflict are types of political violence that eclipse crimes against humanity, genocide and transnational terrorism in terms of human casualties, material destruction and the potential for producing systemic transformation across the international order. I ask: can war, a much-contested concept, really be problematized in such a way that divorces it from the more mundane practices of everyday political life? To answer that question, I canvass several concepts of war before proposing a novel way of thinking about this phenomenon that differs from those conventional approaches which treat "war" as a synonym for either "state aggression" or "armed conflict," or both. I draw on Foucault's notion of silent war to propose that politics is best understood as an extension of the use of armed force before suggesting that the modernist project is the continuation of politico-cultural war. I argue that the *problem of war* lies in the practices of those individuals and groups who, struggling with one another to govern contemporary world affairs, tend to keep questions of state aggression and armed conflict bracketed from the routine politics of international life in part to demonstrate the value of their own roles and responsibilities and to preserve their associated privileges.

Building on my first chapter's concern with political violence, I explore four relatively distinct but interconnecting fields of law that emerge as partial and ongoing responses to that violence and as a potential antidote to the harms which that violence generates. My second chapter shows that international law not only prohibits and, in some cases, criminalizes certain uses of armed force, but also authorizes, and imposes limits on, the use of such force by states and state agents. While these laws of political violence are often treated as separate systems or branches of public international law by legal scholars and practitioners, I believe they are better understood from a politico-analytical perspective as artifacts produced by relatively distinct, but at times interconnecting, social fields in the sense meant by Bourdieu. I suggest these fields tend to emerge and evolve through a transversal dynamic that cuts across horizontal interstate conduct occurring at the international level and across states' vertical reach into their respective domestic domains, a dynamic spurred on through the drafting and negotiation of certain instruments of international law, the implementation and administration of those instruments by state parties, and the monitoring and enforcement of state compliance relating to any duties and responsibilities flowing from those instruments. I offer a brief overview of four fields of law that aim to regulate unruly political violence: namely, the general prohibition on the aggressive use of armed force in international affairs; international humanitarian law; international criminal law and transnational criminal law. Signaling key struggles occurring within these fields, I warn of the dangers associated with the misuse of various instruments of international law which frame the possibilities for, and the limitations of, regulating various types of political violence. I argue the *trouble with international law* is that the most serious struggles occurring within these social fields are determined by configurations of power that are largely external to those fields while the use of armed force continues to entrench a paradigm of control that materially benefits those who live in the zones of privilege found in the Global North and in certain enclaves of the Global South.

I begin my final chapter by noting the emergence of human rights is closely connected to the outbreak of several major wars while the value placed on these rights has been recognized in international law since the Universal Declaration of Human Rights was adopted by the UN General Assembly in 1948. I situate the promotion and protection of human rights within the modernist project before refocusing at the scale of the human species within the epoch of the Anthropocene. With an eye to an ever-darkening horizon, I acknowledge that the politico-cultural project of modernity is based on, and sustained by, routines of domination and exploitation, which manifest not only as violence among groups, communities and societies but also as violence used by humans against other non-human species, plant life and the environment more generally. Drawing on Latour's critique of political ecology, I argue that the *tragedy of human rights* unfolds as actions, taken in the name of advancing and protecting these rights within contemporary world affairs, place humanity in ever greater peril precisely because such actions are driven by an anthropocentric commitment that crowds out regard of, and care for, other life forms and life systems. I end this chapter by pleading for the right to life of non-human species to be taken seriously and more strongly respected in practices of international political life.

I close out this book with a brief conclusion that calls for the academic discipline of International Relations to broaden and deepen its focus beyond its current preoccupation with the state, the economy and society, and transform itself into a misanthropic study of the conduct of contemporary world affairs.

References

Adler-Nissen R, ed. (2013) Bourdieu in International Relations: Rethinking Key Concepts in IR. Routledge, London and New York.

Bigo D (2011) Pierre Bourdieu and International Relations: Power of Practices, Practices of Power. International Political Sociology 5: 225–258.

Bonditti P, Bigo D, and Gros F, eds. (2017) Foucault and the Modern International: Silences and Legacies for the Study of World Politics. Palgrave Macmillan, New York.

Dillon, M and Neal A, eds. (2008) Foucault on Politics, Security and War. Palgrave, New York and London.

Gray J (2007) Black Mass: Apocalyptic Religion and the Death of Utopia. Penguin, London.

Jabre V (2007) Michel Foucault's Analytics of War: The Social, the International, and the Racial. International Political Sociology 1(1): 67–81, https://doi.org/10.1111/j.1749-5687.2007.00005.

Jackson P (2009) Pierre Bourdieu. In Critical Theorists and International Relations, eds. Edkins J and Vaughan-Williams N, 102–113. Routledge, London and New York.

Neal AW (2009) Michael Foucault. In Critical Theorists and International Relations, eds. Edkins J and Vaughan-Williams N, 161–170. Routledge, London and New York.

Pettman R (2001) World Politics: Rationalism and Beyond. Palgrave, New York.

Pettman R (2010) World Affairs: An Analytical Overview. World Scientific, Singapore.

Tarnas R (1991) The Passion of the Western Mind: Understanding the Ideas That Have Shaped Our World View. Pimlico, London.

Toulmin S (1990) Cosmopolis: The Hidden Agenda of Modernity. University of Chicago Press, Chicago.

CHAPTER 2

The Problem of War

Abstract The phenomenon of war is a foundational problem for analysts of contemporary world affairs, not in the philosophical sense that it speaks to some theory of knowledge, as foundationalists like René Descartes would have us do, but rather in the sense that it is a condition of possibility that gives rise to the modernist project and continues to shape its key characteristics—namely, the states-based system, capitalism and the widespread use of reason as an end unto itself—as those characteristics, in turn, reshape war. When analysts provide accounts of war, in all its complexity, they encounter significant empirical obstacles and conceptual difficulties. As types of political violence, state aggression and armed conflict eclipse crimes against humanity, genocide and transnational terrorism in terms of human casualties, material destruction and the potential for producing systemic transformation across the international order, though each of these constitutes an enduring and unruly problem for those who seek to govern contemporary world affairs. Yet can war, a much-contested concept, really be problematized in such a way that divorces it from the more mundane practices of everyday political life? In this chapter, I canvass several concepts of war before proposing a novel way of thinking about this phenomenon that differs from those conventional approaches which treat "war" as a synonym for either "state aggression" or "armed conflict," or both. I draw on Michel Foucault's notion of silent war to propose that politics is best

D. Rogers, *Wars, Laws, Rights and the Making of Global Insecurities*, Human Rights Interventions,
https://doi.org/10.1007/978-3-030-90162-2_2

understood as an extension of the use of armed force before suggesting that the modernist project is the continuation of politico-cultural war. I conclude by warning that those individuals and groups struggling among one another to govern contemporary world affairs keep questions of war separate from the routine politics of international life as means of demonstrating the value of their own roles and responsibilities and of preserving their associated privileges.

Keywords State aggression · Armed conflict · Crimes against humanity · Genocide · Terrorism · Michel Foucault

Political Violence and Human Insecurity

Sources of human insecurity exist in multiple and sometimes evolving forms. Insecurity can stem from anxiety over the unexpectedness of natural disasters—such as earthquakes, volcanic eruptions, tsunamis, hurricanes, tornadoes, typhoons, bush fires and of course pandemics—and an appreciation of their potential to cause destruction and havoc. Insecurity can also result from fear of human-made violence and violent death, particularly when armed force (or even the threat of such force) is used deliberately as a means of coercing obedience to a cause or to certain figures and institutions of authority. Human-made violence takes shape not only as the use of armed force by a sovereign state to attack another sovereign state, and as hostilities waged as part of an ongoing armed conflict, but also as crimes against humanity, and genocide, as well as acts of terrorism. For others, such as Johan Gultang and Carl Jacobson (2000), human-made violence can also be embedded in emerging and existing political, economic and social structures which curtail, or in some cases deny, people's ability to satisfy their daily needs and to realize their full potential as human beings. For Michael McKinley, the neoliberal policies of the Global North are profoundly damaging to contemporary world affairs, especially the false promises made to the Global South encouraging so-called developing countries to transition their economies into liberal markets, which is nothing short of "grand strategic fraud" (2007: 14). The effects produced by these politico-economic practices are, for McKinley, a form of political violence akin to war: "The Theatre of Operations, and thus, the Campaign, and thus, even the Front, is everywhere …

The principal casualties are non-combatants, but that, too, is to commit an anachronism because no distinctions are apparent, certainly none are made, in any case, none are possible, because everyone is in the line of fire" (2007: 14).

This chapter pays attention to human-made violence that involves armed force because this source of human insecurity constitutes a political problem that seems endemic to many societies today. Human-made violence using armed force is an urgent political problem in the sense that it constitutes an important type of power and is, therefore, a means of conducting politics among humans. Yet human-made violence using armed force is a political problem also in the sense that its central dynamic entangles states, which often proclaim a monopoly over the legitimate use of armed force, as both problem solvers and as part of the underlying problem itself. As Robert W. Cox explained many years ago, a problem-solving approach:

> takes the world as it finds it, with the prevailing social and power relationships and the institutions into which they are organized, as the given framework for action. The general aim of problem-solving is to make these relationships and institutions work smoothly by dealing effectively with particular sources of trouble. Since the general pattern of institutions and relationships is not called into question, particular problems can be considered in relation to the specialized areas of activity in which they arise. (1984: 261)

Significantly, human-made violence that relies upon the use of armed force against fellow human beings as means of achieving some ends (hereafter "political violence") has been the subject of various state-based responses, including international legal instruments, which are explored in the next chapter.

The collective use of armed force to exercise power over others for some substantive end was an important, though by no means exclusive, factor contributing to the emergence of modernist world affairs. The Mongolian military campaigns of the thirteenth century linked, albeit temporarily, Eastern Asia with Western Eurasia and reverberated across Africa and the Americas, thereby laying the foundations for several world institutions that constitute the modern world order (Adshead 2004). According to Samuel Adshead, the global arsenal was itself one of the three foundational world institutions, evident in "the merging of separate equestrian styles, the adoption across Eurasia of composite armies of horse, foot and artillery and the articulation of transoceanic sea-power beginning with the voyages of Cheng Ho" (2004: xii). The collective use of armed force also played important role in the construction of the European states system (Tilly 1992), which emerged out of the carnage of the continent's religious wars of the seventeenth century and forms a fundamental element of the Westphalian peace (Wilson 2009). The collective use of armed force also stimulated successive waves of colonialization emanating from Europe since the time of Christopher Columbus and Vasco de Gama throughout the age of empire up until, and including, the so-called War on Terror (Bull and Watson 1984; Barkawi and Stanski 2012). Thus, the collective use of armed force accompanied the rise and spread of the modern state-based system (Sandberg 2016) and its cognate rule of modern international law, and continues to shape the development of both (Black 2015; Chinkin and Kaldor 2017).

Types of Political Violence

The use of armed force by a state to attack, then invade and occupy the territory of another state—that is, state aggression—remains an enduring and unruly problem for those individuals and groups seeking to govern contemporary world affairs. Attacking another state generates a plethora of immediate and lasting impacts, including killing and injuring combatants and civilians, destroying infrastructure required to support the life of populations, and the displacement of those populations to areas beyond the conflict zone. Such attacks invite reprisals too. Conquest, occupation or annexation have led to the destruction and disappearance, or "death," of many states since the beginning of the nineteenth century (Fazal 2007), as well as to regime change within states. In addition to these somewhat localized consequences, which may involve redrawing certain boundaries inscribed on the world map, state aggression can also challenge status quo arrangements by seeking to revise the terms of the overarching international order. Scholars of peace routinely lament the massive cost of this militaristic aspect of international political life, citing, for instance, the diversion of scarce resources toward unnecessary military ends (Cortright 2008). Moreover, the invention of atomic weapons, following the scientific discoveries of the Manhattan Project in the middle of the twentieth century, raised the stakes for all of humanity when an act of state aggression involves a nuclear-armed state. The grim prospect of a nuclear exchange resulting in a kind of species-wide suicide, or self-annihilation, caused much anxiety throughout the Cold War and produced a balance of terror, the legacies of which persist today (Weapons of Mass Destruction Commission 2006; United Nations 2018; see also Munster and Sylvest 2016). An act of state aggression leading to thermonuclear war would, in fact, almost certainly conclude all of the political problems dogging contemporary world affairs by ending struggles among humans for all time.

Political violence seldom recoils from the edges of state aggression. Too often, those acts of aggression transmute into situations of armed conflict; that is, sustained hostilities waged by state militaries and, in many cases, by armed non-state groups. However, the changing characteristics of armed conflict over the course of the twentieth and twenty-first centuries tends to render the distinction between international and non-international armed conflict increasingly less meaningful. Even the distinction between armed conflict as a political act and armed conflict as organized criminality has become increasingly murky (Kaldor 2001). Confusion can exist too over precisely when armed conflicts begin and end, especially when those involved in hostilities experience high levels of violence in the immediate aftermath of armed conflict. Few wars are, moreover, declared nowadays. As a type of political violence, armed conflict sometimes involves the use of excessive military force or results in unintended harms to human beings, their cultural and religious artifacts and the wider environment. Bearing the brunt of contemporary armed conflict, civilians become casualties not just as collateral damage but also as intended targets (Crawford 2015). Recent armed conflicts include the use of child soldiers too, undermining the human potential of an entire generation (Wessells 2006; Dallaire 2010). While death, displacement and devastation are commonplace companions to armed conflict, armed conflict can also result in the changing of political leaders, ruling regimes and political systems, as well as in the destruction or disintegration of states. Significantly, the prevalence and persistence of armed conflict can help normalize recourse to armed force as a means of resolving disputes within contemporary world affairs.

While armed conflict occurring among, between and within sovereign states undoubtedly creates conditions enabling the commission of mass atrocity, crimes against humanity and genocide can also occur beyond such situations. Sometimes these mass atrocities spill across borders, turning localized violence into wider, more complex regional emergencies. In these situations, state capacity to enforce the rule of law can be seriously eroded. Cultures of impunity can arise and sometimes flourish where state leaders are unable, or unwilling, to prevent or curtail the mayhem, provoking intense fear within entire populations and sparking large-scale internal displacement and refugees flows across borders. Yet crimes against humanity, and genocide are types of political violence that often require the organizational capability of a state. State leaders have used the armed force at their disposal to target, rather than to protect, their own citizens. Framed as an international security problem, these atrocities are in some ways worse than state aggression and armed conflict, and deserve to be treated seriously by the international community (Goldhagen 2009). As a type of political violence, crimes against humanity and genocide can be understood as a politico-social problem (Rogers 2018) because certain social groups become targets of armed force and other forms of lethal violence and intense suffering for no more than being who they are, as opposed to some act that they may have committed. This targeting of social groups has dire consequences for human diversity, particularly when they are destroyed as an intended result. The cruel nature of the acts comprising this type of political violence is so heinous that our status as human beings is thereby diminished (Robertson 2008), and is unimaginable and sufficiently repugnant to shock the conscience of humankind (Schabas 2012).

While the term "terrorism" is, for some, a synonym for all types of political violence in the long aftermath of the French Revolution, it is better defined as "a deliberate attempt by a group or by a government regime to create a climate of extreme fear to intimidate a target social group or government or commercial organization with the aim of forcing it to change its behavior. It is generally directed at a wider target than the immediate victims and inherently involves attacks on random or symbolic targets, including civilians" (Wilkinson 2010: 129). Acts of transnational terrorism can be understood as armed revolts from the political margins of world affairs (Rogers 2016), though not all acts of terrorism are created equal. The acts of terrorism, like those seen on 11 September 2001, target civilians but create levels of harm that resemble a full-scale military attack and warrant the label "mega-terrorism" (Falk 2003: 7–8). Sufficiently grave in its impact, the terrorist attacks on the World Trade Centre in New York City, along with its corollary attack on the Pentagon in Washington, DC, provided the *casus belli* for the War on Terror. A sustained campaign led by the US, this War on Terror included armed attacks on Afghanistan and Iraq by US military forces but also involved intelligence agencies and police forces throughout the world. While state aggression and armed conflict produce far more fatalities than these acts deliberately targeting civilians (Zehfuss 2018), the phenomenon of terrorism shows that political violence begets political violence.

Worthy of mention here, too, are the merchants of death who facilitate the transfer of various tools of violence into the hands of those who use them. Amnesty International usefully defines arms brokering as:

> activity carried out by individuals or companies to mediate, arrange or facilitate an international arms transaction between a buyer and seller in return for a fee or material reward. Brokering activity does not necessarily involve the actual purchase, possession or delivery of the arms directly by the brokering agent, although this is often linked in practice. Rather, the brokering activities focus on mediation and may include the provision of vital technical, logistical and financial information to customers about arms suppliers and prospective clients and sub-contractor in different countries, the facilitation of documentation and/or payment between buyer and seller, and/or the arrangement of transportation, finance or insurance services for the delivery of the arms cargo in question. (2006: 58)

Like regulated arms brokers, arms traffickers can, in some cases, stimulate and fuel the abovementioned types of political violence. Unlike their regulated counterparts, however, traffickers organize their business dealings in such a way as to place themselves beyond the reach of law enforcement agencies and circumvent existing arms control measures, including arms embargoes contained within sanction regimes authorized by the UN Security Council. In order to ply their trade to those who use armed force to achieve their objectives, these black-market merchants rely on false information, fraudulent documents, complex business arrangements, alternative currencies and so-called "flags of convenience" (Rogers 2009). Arms traffickers can take more active measures too, bribing customs officers to "look the other way" (Lumpe 2000). Where such incentives prove insufficient, the threat of armed force is never far away. These merchants of death use the threat of force to coerce others while they themselves contribute in vital ways to the widespread availability and ongoing use of small arms and light weapons, the primary tools of political violence in contemporary world affairs. While drug smuggling, people smuggling and human trafficking can follow social upheavals and population displacements caused by state aggression, armed conflict, crimes against humanity and genocide, the illicit transfer of small arms and light weapons is a transnational practice that enables the use of armed force. For that reason, firearms trafficking receives mention in this chapter, ahead of other nefarious transnational activities, such as people smuggling, human trafficking and drug trafficking.

Understanding the Fury of War

While each type of political violence constitutes an enduring and unruly problem for those who seek to govern contemporary world affairs, state aggression and armed conflict—generally understood as elements comprising "war"—eclipse crimes against humanity, genocide and transnational terrorism in terms of human mortality, material destruction and the potential for producing systemic transformation across the international order. The heart of war beats to the killing of human beings, though it is the centrifugal destructiveness of war's fury, once unleashed, that renders it the most serious type of political violence. War's direct impacts include the deliberate and wanton death and injury inflicted upon combatants and civilians alike, the displacement of populations and the creation of refugees, and the destruction of urban and rural habitats alongside the devastation of broader environments. Other casualties of war include damage to, if not the destruction of, cultural and religious monuments that lend life meaning for many human beings, the diversion of material resources otherwise intended to aid human progress, and the reinforcing of a norm where the use of armed force is accepted and the militarized conduct of world affairs remains entrenched.

The trauma of experiencing the horrors of war will continue to haunt war fighters and their victims long after the fighting has ceased. When Henry Dunant, one of the founders of the International Committee of the Red Cross, witnessed the immediate aftermath of the Battle of Solferino in 1859, he described the human carnage in the grisliest terms possible while lamenting that humanity's capacity to inflict harm and suffering on fellow human beings would only be increased by "the new and frightful weapons of destructions which are now at the disposal of nations" (Dunant 1939: 128). It was a prophetic vision. In short, as a type of political violence wars are an especially morbid phenomenon that generates immediate and lasting human misery on a massive scale, establishing and sustaining sets of deplorable conditions under which significant portions of humanity are prevented from flourishing. It is a phenomenon that can alter the structures of the everyday politics of international life.

Despite curbing humanity's potential, some analysts are quick to proclaim war's transformative and restorative virtue. Some, for instance, see war as an opportunity to obtain gains otherwise unachievable. War-making is sometimes promoted as a means of protecting existing, or obtaining additional, territories, an opportunity for fostering a warrior class and transforming individual soldiers into heroes, and an occasion to galvanize the state, the economy and society in the pursuit of a totalizing objective. Preparation for war can also involve research and development efforts that result in technological advancements, including Global Positioning Satellite technologies and, of course, the Internet, two war-related technologies that now feature in everyday use among those of us living in the Global North. Moreover, war can unleash revolutions against tyrannical rule and colonial oppression as means of achieving political independence and greater measures of liberty and freedom. For Edward Luttwak, war's great virtue lies in its ability to resolve political disputes and establish peaceful relations by one party of a conflict prevailing over others through force of arms, or all belligerents reaching a level of exhaustion that they can no longer sustain. "War brings peace," Luttwak argues, "only after passing a culminating phase of violence" (1999: 36).

Putting aside debates over war's virtues and vices, today's accounts of war's causes, conduct and consequences have deep roots, some of which date back to the earliest human records. Great historians of the classical era—Herodotus and Thucydides, Julius Caesar and Livy, as well as non-Europeans Sun Tzu and Ibn Khaldun to name but a few—chronicled war as though it were a macabre motor of history. Sometimes referred to as polemology, War Studies is less its own discrete academic discipline and more a distinct field of inquiry subjected to various disciplinary-specific examinations. These disciplines include History, particularly military history, Political Science, International Relations, Philosophy, Social Anthropology, Sociology, Geography, Law and Literature, among others. Although disciplinary-specific inquiry tends to examine certain aspects of war in a way that illuminates some other pre-existing disciplinary concern, thereby "decentering" war (Barkawi and Brighton 2011: 256), each disciplinary perspective has, nonetheless, significant potential to produce reliable knowledge on, and to advance our collective understanding of, the very important phenomenon of war.

Several research institutes collect, store and analyze information pertaining to war, thereby functioning as crucial repositories of war data. Foremost among these is the Correlates of War Project, based at Pennsylvania State University. It aims to enable the gathering, dissemination and free public use of accurate and reliable data sets on war.[1] Another important repository is the Conflict Data Program hosted by Sweden's Uppsala University and the Peace Research Institute, Oslo in Norway. It provides high-quality data on organized violence around the world, including information on civil wars, which are comparable across cases, countries and years.[2] According to the UCDP data, there was a decreasing number of people killed by organized violence during 2018, though this decline in morbidity rates does not mean the number of active conflicts also fell. The number of active conflicts in the world has, in fact, increased since 2014 (Petterrson et al. 2019). More recent estimates are gloomy. The trend of declining fatalities from organized violence was broken in 2020 as UCDP registered more than 80,100 deaths in 2020, compared to 76,300 in 2019. The US departure from Afghanistan could see these numbers grow. The number of active armed conflict has increased too since 2019 (Petterrson et al. 2021). War, it seems, remains deadly and widespread, and shows few signs of abating.

War analysts draw upon a wide range of other sources, including their own observations, interviews, official records, nongovernmental reports, media coverage as well as scholarly work in order to help them produce knowledge and thereby advance understanding of this complex phenomenon. Despite the fecundity of war data, making sense of war continues to pose an array of empirical challenges, however. For starters, calculating injury, displacement and mortality rates among combatants and civilians with any degree of certainty is fraught with practical difficulties and proximal dangers. On the ground, combatants wearing uniforms and openly carrying arms are relatively easy to identify when compared to those individuals or groups supporting conflicts from behind the scenes or from afar, though as hostilities unfold the distinction between combatants and civilians can become blurred, sometimes deliberately (Crawford 2015). Commanders' strategic intentions can evolve in unforeseen directions too and are easily misinterpreted. Symptoms of strife can easily be mistaken for root causes, as can events triggering resort to armed force. Lulls in fighting can be misconstrued as ceasefires and ceasefires as peace. Post-conflict situations can carry levels of armed violence at least as intense as those experienced by civilians during low-intensity hostilities, thereby undermining formal declarations of conflict cessation. The rebuilding of war-ravaged communities in the image of occupying forces can undermine any surviving sense of collective identity, perpetuating and intensifying grievances of the vanquished. For analysts concerned with making sense of war, reliable information is frequently patchy and highly provisional, though rumor, speculation and misinformation are usually found in abundance. Despite such empirical challenges, war analysts remain preoccupied with providing meaningful accounts of war in all its complexity.

When it comes to providing accounts of strife, states stand out as the primary entities of analytic concern for many war analysts. This is for good reason because, as Charles Tilly (1992) argued, war played a major role in developing the modern state while the state itself played a major role in making war modern. Analysts sometimes stretch the notion of the state to include state-like entities which follow discernable war-related policy objectives (Schabas 2012). However, complicating matters for war analysts are those non-state groups and super-empowered individuals lacking any desire to adorn themselves in sovereign robes in the sense meant by James Rosenau when he wrote that "states are conceived to be *sovereignty–bound* actors, while multinational corporations, ethnic groups, bureaucratic agencies, political parties, subnational governments, transnational societies, international organizations and a host of other types of collectivities are called *sovereignty-free* actors" (1990: 36). In terms of fueling political violence, such sovereignty-free actors include small arms manufacturers, arms merchants, traders and traffickers and the logistics companies that support them as well as mercenaries, private security firms and security consultancies, to name but a pernicious few. Furthermore, the doctrine of individual responsibility (with its teeth first sharpened at the Nuremberg trials in the mid-1940s), as well as the groups protected under the Geneva Conventions of 1947 and its subsequent protocols of 1977 (namely, the sick and wounded on land and at seas, prisoners of war, and civilians) and under the Convention on the Prevention and Punishment of the Crime of Genocide of 1948 (namely, groups based on nationality, ethnicity religion or race) also pose a significant challenge to the conceptual primacy afforded to states in certain accounts of war, as does the entire human security agenda that emerged in the aftermath of the Cold War.

This prioritization of the state means that war analysts typically discern two categories of war: international armed conflict and non-international armed conflict. By the former, they usually mean situations where armed force is used as a coercive means between or among states. By the latter, they usually mean situations where armed force is used as a coercive means between one state and one or more armed non-state groups contesting the legitimacy of that state's monopoly over the use of force within a particular jurisdiction (or, in the absence of a functioning state, then contestation among armed non-state groups). The latter is often referred to as a civil war or internal armed conflict, though as Rod Alley (2004) observes these wars' causes, conduct and consequences are not easily comprehended outside the world of international relations and its diplomatic practices. Significantly, it makes very little difference to victims' direct experience of war, and its attendant miseries, if that war is categorized by analysts as either an international or a non-international armed conflict. These binary categories are easily problematized, moreover. The line between domestic riots or internal disturbances and civil war is easily drawn, but sometimes difficult to sustain. One reason for this is levels of armed force and other forms of deadly violence in global megacities, such as Rio de Janerio, Johannesburg and Los Angeles, create casualty lists that are on par with some civil wars (see, for instance, Peres 2004). Problematic too is the specter of war-like violence, particularly the commission of crimes against humanity and genocide, which can occur without a nexus to a situation of either international or non-international armed conflict. Furthermore, there are certain conditions under which armed conflicts between groups fighting within a state's sovereign territory are understood not so much as civil war, but rather, as an *internationalized* armed conflict: key determinants here include the set of circumstances in which belligerent groups obtain international recognition as parties to an armed conflict, whether or not the purpose of war is a group's self-determination and, one rare occasions, if the UN has authorized and sent intervening forces.

Scholars have advanced our collective understanding of war by identifying and explaining its "essential" characteristics. Resource wars, for instance, involve the collective use of armed force (or the threat of such force) to obtain or retain control over water, oil and natural gases, each a vital ingredient in fueling modern industrialized economies, though access to minerals, gems and timber is increasingly sought as sources of wealth (Klare 2002). While ethnic wars are fought along specific social cleavages, cosmopolitan wars involve groups of individuals who, fighting over collective social and political ends, are agents whose acts of killing as combatants need justifying just as much as the suffering of civilians (Fabre 2012). Religious wars are understood as "an extended act of eschatological and cataclysmic violence executed within the authorizing power of self-anointed messianism … At the heart of them all is some dogma demanding absolute allegiance and exclusivity—effectively, the surrender of conscience and judgement—in the name of a reigning divinity or truth" (McKinley 2007: 216–217). Irregular wars are now understood in light of an asymmetric power relationship that produces organized violence sparked and sustained by two separate but closely intertwined factors: growing inequality within and between societies; and human-made climate changes that degrade the planet (Rogers 2016). New wars involve the mixing of armed force deployed by states and state-like groups for public objectives with unlawful armed violence controlled by organized crime groups for private financial benefit (Kaldor 2001; Chinkin and Kaldor 2017). There are, it seems, as many forms of war as there are essential characteristics of war.

While war is understood as an all-too-common and highly-lethal form of political violence that constitutes a serious security challenge to the conduct of contemporary world affairs, there is considerable debate over what, exactly, is meant by the term "war." There is no consensus on the precise content of the concept of war, or where its limits lie. John Vasquez (2009) provides a useful survey of different understandings of war from some of the world's great thinkers. For Cicero, one of the great Roman orators, war is simply "contending by force" (30) whereas Lewis Richardson understands war to be a "deadly quarrel," a specific kind of killing which stems from basic human aggression. War is, for Hedley Bull, organized violence unleashed by political units against one another while Bronislaw Malinowski goes further by describing war as "an armed contest between two independent political units, by means of organized military force, in the pursuit of a tribal or national policy" (24). For Hugo Grotius, the father of modern international law, war is not a contest but "a legal condition" (30–31). Building on these ideas, Quincy Wright suggested that war is "the legal condition which equally permits two or more hostile groups to carry on a conflict by armed force" (31). Margaret Mead argues that war is "a social invention that gives people the idea that war is the way certain situations are to be handled … is learned behavior… [and the] learning is collective (32–33). In other words, war is socially constructed. For the early modern political philosopher Thomas Hobbes, war was not simply the act of fighting battles, but also included the threat of performing such an action where no guarantees to the contrary were given (39). Having offered this survey, Vasquez himself then suggested "that war as an institution is a form of force that has evolved within the global political system as a unilateral allocation mechanism that can make authoritative decisions. War is not simply an act of violence, but an allocative mechanism which is resorted to in the face of stalemate and the failure of normal politics to resolve fundamental issues" (52).

Even though war remains an essentially contested concept and, by corollary, making sense of war continues to be deeply problematic, there is a weak but broad consensus that war requires at least two or more political actors whose relationship is structured by armed force. By political actors, I mean here any institutions, groups or communities that seek to obtain and maintain power over others for non-trivial purposes.[3] This notion of war is expansive, embracing not merely belligerents, their actions and their victims, but also the full panoply of individuals and groups involved in stimulating and enabling the violence, as well as those non-belligerents seeking to ameliorate the suffering of those in harm's way. This notion, however, excludes Johan Galtung's notion of structural violence which, depending upon "inequality" and "exploitation" as social and economic relations, prevents much of humanity from fulfilling its potential (Galtung and Jacobsen 2000: 270).

Foucault's Silent War

Notwithstanding these complexities, understanding war as a clash of arms during battle, or a series of battles, fought among state-makers (including prospective state-makers) found clear expression in the work of the Prussian soldier Carl von Clausewitz who, responding to his experience of the Napoleonic wars, famously wrote that war is a mere continuation of policy by other means. Clausewitz posited that:

> We see, therefore, that War is not merely a political act, but also a real political instrument, a continuation of political commerce, a carrying out of the same by other means. All beyond this which is strictly peculiar to War relates merely to the peculiar nature of the means which the Art of War in general and the Commander in each particular case may demand, and this claim is truly not a trifling one. But however powerfully this may

> react on political views in particular cases, still it must always be regarded as only a modification of them; for the political view is the object, War is the means, and the means must always include the object in our conception. (1982: 119)

By this, Clausewitz meant that war was politics—diplomacy, specifically—conducted by other means and that the use of armed force followed the exhaustion, or failure, of political efforts. It is a formulation that found a wide audience, though some take issue with it (see Keegan 1993). War is, thus, bracketed away from routine politics as a form of anti-politics or, at the very least, given status as a specialized form of exceptional politics with its own rules, norms and meanings. Yet can war really be problematized in such a way that divorces it from the more mundane practices of everyday political life?

For Michel Foucault, Clausewitz's statements could not stand uncontested. During a lecture series at the College de France in 1976, Foucault inverted Clausewitz's well-known dictum, suggesting instead that politics is the continuation of war by other means because relationships of "politicised" power emerged from relationships of armed force established through conflicts occurring at particular places and times. These new power relations help to transform a condition of conflict into a condition of peace, preserving the result of conflict in a "sort of silent war" that enshrines (uneven) relationships of force, re-inscribing that relationship in institutions, economic inequalities, social relations language and, in some cases, individuals bodies. Such a peace masks the ongoing "political" rivalries over access to power which are best understood "as so many episodes, fragmentation and displacements of the war itself. We are always writing the history of the same war, even when we are writing the history of peace and its institutions" (Foucault 2003: 15–16). Although Foucault did not systemically explore the consequences of his inversion of Clausewitz's dictum, moving on into his investigations of biopolitics, biopower and governmentality, the implications of his inversion remain profound for war analysts. As Julian Reid puts it:

> [w]ar figures ultimately for Foucault not as a primitive state of being against which modern societies and their power relations can be differentiated, not simply as a utile instrument for the pursuit of the grand strategies of state in paradoxical compromise of the civil condition of

> modern societies, but rather, as a 'condition of possibility' for the constitution of modern power relations in which the aleatory conditions of species life is variably recruited, set free, manipulated and put to work in the development of modern social arrangements. (2008: 66)

For the purposes of this book, Foucault's inversion of Clausewitz gives rise to four closely related implications for analysts interested in better understanding and explaining war's conditions, dynamics and legacies (Rogers 2018).

Firstly, the recast relationship between war and politics can be viewed through a narrow, state-based lens, as Foucault aptly demonstrated. But it can also be viewed through a wider focus on the broader, deeper and altogether more profound politico-cultural project of modernity. Adopting a politico-cultural lens enables us to better comprehend the thirteenth-century Mongolian explosion as a sustained campaign of armed force, or what Samuel Adshead described as "the big bang of world history" (2004: xii) that created the pre-conditions needed for the rise of major world institutions. Together, these world institutions—namely, the basic information circuit on geography and history; the global arsenal and related military techniques; the religious internationalists; the world market for currency, commodities and capital; the secular republic of letters and sciences and, perhaps most urgently today, the microbian common market of disease—constitute the nascent modern international order. It enables us, moreover, to better comprehend Europe's religious wars of the seventeenth century as various campaigns of armed force, but which, concluding with the treaties of Westphalia, laid the basis of the current states-based system of world affairs. It also enables us to also understand the First and Second World Wars as campaigns of armed force that led to the establishment of the League of Nations in the first instance, and the United Nations, International Monetary Fund and the World Bank in the second instance. These international organizations, alongside the international rule of law, are key institutions used to govern the conduct of contemporary international life. The politics of modernist world affairs emergences from, and is shaped by, successive armed conflicts of global significance. The phenomenon of war is thus a foundational problem for analysts of contemporary world affairs. It is a foundational problem but not in the philosophical sense that it speaks to some theory of knowledge, as foundationalists like René Descartes would have us do. But rather, in the sense that it is a condition of possibility that gives rise to the modernist project and continues to shape its key characteristics—namely, the states-based system, capitalism and the widespread use of reason as an end unto itself—as those characteristics, in turn, reshape war.

Secondly, appreciating that war begets politics behooves us to reimagine war's usual province. The modern battlespace is no longer understood as some geographically bounded area in which militaries contend through demonstrations of armed force, but rather, is now understood as the main politico-strategic, politico-economic and politico-social dimensions of world affairs. In other words, modernist politics erupts into a new imaginary battlespace for control over states, over states and their economies, and over states and their economies and societies. As such, an overarching intent of much modernist politics is to obtain control over the architecture of the politico-cultural project, that is, the institutions of global reach that govern, to greater or lesser degrees, the world's state-making, market-making and self-making practices.

Thirdly, the Foucauldian inversion of Clausewitz invites us to reconsider the assemblages within our often taken-for-granted political ontologies; modernist politics is not only fought for control over politico-cultural projects but it is also waged by proponents of modernity's contending utopian movements. These utopian movements are not necessarily aligned in accordance with particular states, though as Martti Koskenniemi reminds us, "economists, environmentalists, and human rights experts are just as divided among themselves as Finns, Frenchmen, or Fijians about how to understand the world and what to do with it" (2011: 69). Key examples of utopian movements from the twentieth and twenty-first centuries include Nazism, Shinto-Imperialism, Soviet-styled Communism, Neoliberalism, Christo-Slavism, Hutu supremacy and Islamic fundamentalism, each by-product of the European enlightenment and the modernist project. As amalgams of nationalism, ethnicity, race, class or religion, these movements use various types of political violence—that is, state aggression, armed conflict, crimes against humanity, genocide and transnational terrorism—as a means of radically remaking society. However, as Gray warns, these utopias can never be realized, but are, instead, "[dreams of collective deliverance that in waking life are found to be nightmares" (2007: 17).

Fourthly, war-induced politics illustrates the changing character of political violence. In this regard, modernist politics represents a transformation of wars' routine conduct. The formal cessation of hostilities becomes less meaningful when power relations transcend the clash of arms during battle. War is now silent and insidious, using the threat of armed force to underscore and animate a politics that pacifies dissent, protest and criticism through various institutions, values, norms and practices. It relies on various techniques and apparatuses of control over knowledge production, social norms and the respect of the rule of law, giving rise to "lawfare" where international law is used as an "increasingly powerful and prevalent weapon of war" (Kittrie 2016: 1). This includes the development and enforcement of international criminal law, which some critics have described as victors' justice (Minear 1971), as well as international humanitarian law and transnational criminal law. This is, perhaps, what Herfried Munkler (2012) might describe as wars of pacification, though, perhaps, on a more grand and extended scale than he imagined.

Conclusion

For Hannah Arendt, violence is an instrument of power and is not power itself, and "to use them as synonyms not only indicates a certain deafness to linguistic meanings, which would be serious enough, but it has also resulted in a kind of blindness to the realities they correspond to" (1970: 238). War, too, is an imperfect synonym for state aggression and armed conflict. It is much more than a clash of arms by military forces engaged in the heat of battle or sustained over longer campaigns, though the coercive use of armed force, and the threat of such force, remain central to war's fury. That forms of organized violence, transformed into modernist politics, are often silent and insidious makes it no less powerful, destructive, oppressive, morbid, brutal and traumatizing. Furthermore, this relatively novel understanding of war highlights the involvement of groups that go well beyond the obvious belligerents let loose by state-makers, whose own conduct is at times shaped by the aspirations of various utopian movements. The problem of war, I suggest, is to be found in the practices of those individuals and groups who, struggling among one another to govern contemporary world affairs, keep questions of war separate from the routine politics of international life, otherwise their roles, responsibilities and associated privileges would be placed at great risk of becoming irrelevant.

Notes

1. "About the Correlates of War project," https://correlatesofwar.org (accessed 8 January 2020).
2. "About UCDP," https://www.pcr.uu.se/research/ucdp/about-ucdp (accessed 8 January 2020).
3. This definition of politics is derived from one offered by Pettman (2001).

References

Adshead SAM (2004) T'ang China: The Rise of the East in World History. Palgrave Macmillan, New York.

Alley R (2004) Internal Conflict and the International Community: Wars Without End? Ashgate, Aldershot.

Amnesty International (2006) Dead on Time—Arms Transportation, Brokering and the Threat to Human Rights. International Secretariat, London.

Arendt H (1970) On Violence. Harcourt, Brace and World.

Barkawi T and Brighton S (2011) Conclusion: Absent War Studies? War, Knowledge, and Critique. In The Changing Character of War, eds. Strachan H and Scheipers S. Oxford University Press, Oxford.

Barkawi T and Stanski K, eds. (2012) Orientalism and War. Hurst & Company, London.

Black J (2015) War in the Modern War, 1990–2014. Routledge, London and New York.

Bull H and Watson A (1984) The Expansion of International Society. Oxford University Press, Oxford.

Chinkin C and Kaldor M (2017) International Law and New Wars. Cambridge University Press, Cambridge.

Clausewitz C (1982; first published 1832) On War. Penguin, London.

Cortright D (2008) Peace: A History of Movements and Ideas. Cambridge University Press, Cambridge.

Cox RW (1984) Social Forces, States and World Orders: Beyond International Relations Theory. In Culture, Ideology, and World Order, ed. Walker RBJ. Westworld Press, Boulder and London.

Crawford E (2015) Identifying the Enemy: Civilian Participation in Armed Conflict. Oxford University Press, Oxford.

Dallaire R (2010) The Fight Like Soldiers, They Die Like Children. Hutchinson, London.

Dunant H (1939) A Memory of Solferino. International Committee of the Red Cross, Geneva, Switzerland.
Fabre C (2012) Cosmopolitan War. Oxford University Press, Oxford.
Falk R (2003). The Great Terror War. Aris Books, Gloucestershire.
Fazal TM (2007) State Death: The Politics and Geography of Conquest, Occupation and Annexation. Princeton University Press, Princeton and Oxford.
Foucault M (2003) "Society Must Be Defended": Lectures at the College de France, 1975–1976, trans. Macey D. Picador, New York.
Galtung J and Jacobsen CG (2000) Searching for Peace: The Road to TRANSCEND. Pluto Press, London and Sterling, Virginia.
Goldhagen DJ (2009) Worse Than War: Genocide, Eliminationism, and the Ongoing Assault on Humanity. Little Brown, London.
Gray J (2007) Black Mass: Apocalyptic Religion and the Death of Utopia. Penguin, London.
Kaldor M (2001) New and Old Wars: Organised Violence in a Global Era. Polity, Cambridge.
Keegan J (1993) A History of Warfare. Random House, London.
Kittrie OF (2016) Lawfare: Law as a Weapon of War. Oxford University Press, Oxford.
Klare MT (2002) Resource Wars: The New Landscape of Global Conflict. Henry Holt and Company, New York.
Koskenniemi M (2011) The Politics of International Law. Hart Publishing, Oxford and Portland, Oregon.
Lumpe L, ed. (2000) Running Guns: The Global Black Market in Small Arms. Zed, London.
Luttwak EN (1999) Give War a Chance. Foreign Affairs 78(4) (July–Aug): 36–44.
McKinley M (2007) Economic Globalization as Religious War: Tragic Convergence. Routledge, London and New York
Minear RH (1971) Victors' Justice: The Tokyo War Crimes Trial. Princeton University Press, New Jersey.
Munkler H (2012) Old and New Wars. In The Routledge Handbook of Security Studies, eds. Cavelty MD and Mauer V, 190–199. Routledge, New York and London.
Peres MFT (2004) Firearm-Related Violence in Brazil: Country Report. Centre for the Study of Violence, University of Sao Paulo.
Petterrson T, Davies S, Deniz A, Engstrom G, Hawach N, Hogbadh S, and Oberg MSM (2021) Organized Violence, 1989–2020, with a Special Focus on Syria. Journal of Peace Research 58(4): 809–825.
Petterrson T, Hogbladh S and Oberg M (2019) Organized Violence, 1989–2018 and Peace Agreements. Journal of Peace Research 56(94): 589–603.
Pettman R (2001) World Politics: Rationalism and Beyond. Palgrave, New York.

Reid J (2008) Life Struggles: War, Discipline and Biopolitics in the Thought of Michel Foucault. In Foucault on Politics, Security and War, eds. Dillon M and Neal AW, 65–92. Palgrave Macmillan, New York.
Robertson G (2008) Crimes Against Humanity: The Struggle for Global Justice. Penguin, London.
Rogers D (2009) Postinternationalism and Small Arms Control: Theory, Politics, Security. Surrey, Ashgate.
Rogers P (2016) Irregular War: ISIS and the New Threat from the Margins. I.B. Tauris, London and New York.
Rogers D (2018) Law, Politics and the Limits of Prosecuting Mass Atrocity. Palgrave Macmillan, New York.
Rosenau JN (1990) Turbulence in World Politics: A Theory of Change and Continuity. Princeton University Press, New Jersey.
Sandberg B (2016) War and Conflict in the Early Modern World, 1500-1700. Polity, Cambridge.
Schabas W (2012) Unimaginable Atrocities: Justice, Politics, and Rights at the War Crimes Tribunals. Oxford University Press, Oxford.
Tilly C (1992) Coercion, Capital, and European States, Ad 990-1992. Blackwell, Cambridge and Oxford.
van Munster R and Sylvest C (2016) Nuclear Realism: Global Political Thought During the Thermonuclear Revolution. Routledge, New York and London.
Vasquez JA (2009) The War Puzzle Revisited. Cambridge University Press, Cambridge.
Wessells M (2006) Child Soldiers: From Violence to Protection. Harvard University Press, Cambridge, Massachusetts.
Wilkinson P (2010) Terrorism. In The Routledge Handbook of Security Studies, eds. Cavelty MD and Mauer V. Routledge, London and New York.
Wilson PH (2009) The Thirty Years War: Europe's Tragedy. Belknap Press of Harvard University Press, Cambridge, Massachusetts.
Zehfuss M (2018) War and the Politics of Ethics. Oxford University Press, Oxford.

Official Reports

United Nations Office for Disarmament Affairs (2018) *Securing Our Common Future: An Agenda for Disarmament.* New York.
Weapons of Mass Destruction Commission (2006) *Weapons of Terror: Freeing the World of Nuclear, Biological and Chemical Arms.* Stockholm.

CHAPTER 3

The Trouble with International Law

Abstract International law not only prohibits and, in some cases, criminalizes certain uses of armed force but also authorizes, and imposes limits on, the use of such force by states and state agents. While these laws of political violence are often treated as separate systems or branches of public international law by legal scholars and practitioners, they are, perhaps from a politico-analytical perspective, better understood as artifacts produced by relatively distinct, but at times interconnecting, social fields in the sense meant by Pierre Bourdieu. These fields tend to emerge and evolve through a transversal dynamic that occurs between horizontal interstate conduct and vertical state reach, a dynamic spurred on through the drafting and negotiation of certain instruments of international law, the implementation and administration of those instruments by state parties, and the monitoring and enforcement of state compliance relating to any duties and responsibilities flowing from those instruments. In this chapter, I offer a brief overview of four fields of law that aim to regulate unruly political violence: namely, the general prohibition on the aggressive use of armed force in international affairs; international humanitarian law; international criminal law and transnational criminal law. I warn of the dangers associated with the misuse of various instruments of international law, arguing that the trouble with international law is that the key struggles over them are often determined by configurations of power that are external to those fields.

D. Rogers, *Wars, Laws, Rights and the Making of Global Insecurities*, Human Rights Interventions,
https://doi.org/10.1007/978-3-030-90162-2_3

Keywords International humanitarian law · International criminal law · Transnational criminal law · Humanity law · Pierre Bourdieu

Bourdieu's Fields of Law

Building on my second chapter, which introduced various types of political violence that constitute enduring and unruly problems for those individuals and groups who seek to govern contemporary world affairs, this third chapter explores four relatively distinct but interconnecting fields of law that emerge as partial and ongoing responses to that violence and as a potential antidote to the various harms which that violence generates. According to Pierre Bourdieu, "a 'field' is an area of structured, socially patterned activity or 'practice'" and a juridical field "is organized around a body of internal protocols and assumptions, characteristic behaviors and self-sustaining values—what we might informally term a 'legal culture'" (Terdiman 1987: 805–806). More specifically, Bourdieu argues that:

> The social practices of the law are in fact the product of the functioning of a 'field' whose specific logic is determined by two factors: on the one hand, by the specific power relations which give it its structure and which order the competitive struggles (or, more precisely, the conflicts over competence) that occur within it; and on the other hand, by the internal logic of juridical functioning which constantly constrains the range of possible actions and, thereby, limits the realm of specifically juridical solutions. (1987: 816)

In so doing, Bourdieu distinguishes a judicial field from a legal system, which is built on self-enclosing legal structures and self-referring legal logics, and from branches belonging to a larger body of knowledge on rules and related practices.[1] Such an intellectual move enables Bourdieu, and followers of his work, to take those structures and logics, as well as that knowledge and practice, as the object of academic inquiry, thereby eschewing the shackles of doctrinal debates taking place among various scholars and practitioners of the law. This approach casts light on the social relationships among these fields of law, the struggles that occur within these fields, and the exterior configurations of power which inform and shape those fields and can, at least partly, determine the outcome of those struggles.

Significantly, the fields of law considered here are concerned not only with prohibiting and criminalizing certain acts relating to the use of armed force but also with authorizing the limited use of such force by states and state agents. While a field of law is constituted in part by various principles and rules relating to the rights and responsibilities of its subjects, there are overarching rules that shape the development of instruments of international law, though the content and applicability of these "secondary rules" can be the subject of dispute (Thirlway 2010). These secondary rules, often referred to as sources of international law, are recognized in Article 38 of the Statute of the International Court of Justice as:

(a) International conventions, whether general or particular, establishing rules expressly recognized by the contesting parties;
(b) International custom, as evidence of a general practice accepted as law;
(c) The general principles of law recognized by civilized nations; and
(d) [...] judicial decisions and the teachings of the most qualified publicists of the various nations, as subsidiary means for the determination of rules of law.

The social fields explored below tend to emerge and evolve through a transversal dynamic that occurs between horizontal interstate conduct and vertical state reach over individuals and groups deemed responsible for political violence attracting international concern. This lawmaking dynamic is spurred on through the drafting and negotiation of certain instruments of international law by state-makers, the implementation and administration of those instruments by state parties and some select others, and the monitoring and enforcement of state compliance relating to any duties and responsibilities flowing from those instruments by various members of the wider international community.

Laws of Political Violence

Prohibition on Aggressive Armed Force

According to Justice Robert Jackson, the lead American prosecutor at the Nuremburg trial of Germany's war-time leaders (1945–1946), state aggression was the supreme international crime. Even though Germany had not breached a peace treaty with the United States, its aggressive use of armed force in Europe was an attack, Jackson insisted, upon the peace enjoyed by the society of states. In his prosecutorial opening statement, Jackson proclaimed state aggression was "the greatest menace of our times" (International Military Tribunal 1947, 99). According to Jackson, "[i]t was aggressive war, which the nations of the world had renounced. It was war in violation of treaties, by which the peace of the world was sought to be safe-guarded" (International Military Tribunal 1947: 104).[2] Joseph B. Keenan, the lead American prosecutor at the Tokyo Trial of Japan's war-time leaders (1946–1948), echoed Jackson's rhetoric when he stated that "our specific purpose is to contribute all we soundly can toward the end—the prevention of the scourge of aggressive war" (Keenan 1946, 1) and "[o]ur purpose is one of prevention or deterrence" and asked: "what can we do with the powers conferred upon us here in this courtroom to contribute in a just and efficient manner to the prevention of future wars?" (3). Starting an international armed conflict, rather than losing one, was the main offense underlying both prosecutions because these acts of state aggression were part of a concerted attempt to revise the prevailing international order, and thereby provided the underlying conditions needed for other heinous crimes of international concern. The bench at both trials generally agreed, finding the prosecution has provided enough evidence to enable them to return numerous verdicts of guilty with respect to the crime against peace.

Both post-war trials were thus important to the development of the general prohibition on the aggressive use of armed force in international affairs, not least because the underlying Charters helped codify the substantive crime in question; specifically, Article 6(a) of the Charter of the International Military Tribunal at Nuremberg declared crimes against peace as "the planning, preparation, initiation or waging of a war of aggression, or a war in violation of international treaties, agreements or assurances, or participation in a common plan or conspiracy for the accomplishment of any of the foregoing" whereas Article 5 of the Charter of the International Military Tribunal for the Far East stated that crimes against peace included "the planning, preparation, initiation or waging of a declared or undeclared war of aggression, or a war in violation of international law, treaties, agreements or assurances or participation in a common plan or conspiracy for the accomplishment of any of the foregoing."

Yet these trials were not the first occasions when an argument was made that state aggression constituted a crime. The first major attempts at criminalizing aggression took place in the aftermath of the First World War when the prosecution of the Kaiser for "a supreme offence against international morality and the sanctity of treaties" (Article 227) was contemplated and found partial expression in Articles 227–231 of the Treaty of Peace Between the Allied and Associated Powers and Germany (1918) (sometimes referred to as the Treaty of Versailles) though, of course, the Kaiser, absconding to The Netherlands, never faced trial (Sellars 2014: 1). Article 231, which is sometimes referred to as the war guilt clause, states: "The Allied and Associated Governments affirm and Germany accepts the responsibility of Germany and her allies for causing all the loss and damage to which the Allied and Associated Governments and their nationals have been subjected as a consequence of the war imposed upon them by the aggression of Germany and her allies." In so doing, the Treaty of Versailles effectively disregarded the presumption of innocence.

Article X of the Covenant of the League of Nations (1919) also stated that "Members of the League undertake to respect and preserve as against external aggression the territorial integrity and existing political independence of all Members of the League. In case of any such aggression or in case of any threat or danger of such aggression the Council shall advise upon the means by which this obligation shall be fulfilled." While the Covenant did not outlaw war, it did seek to place the initiation of international armed conflict under the reach of international law to prevent and deter state-makers from launching armed attacks (Sellars 2014). A decade after the Covenant was agreed, Article 1 of the General Treaty for the Renunciation of War as an Instrument of National Policy (1928) (sometimes referred to as the Kellogg-Briand Pact) stated: "The High Contracting Parties solemnly declare in the names of their respective peoples that they condemn recourse to war for the solution of international controversies, and renounce it, as an instrument of national policy in their relations with one another." The significance of the Kellogg-Briand Pact lies in the way it enables a war to be distinguished as either lawful or unlawful, a distinction which would be required for the criminalization of acts of aggression. The years between the First and Second World Wars were, however, bereft of major development in the laws criminalizing states' aggressive use of armed force in international affairs. As Kirsten Sellars explains:

> Lloyd George's proposal to arraign the ex-Kaiser for starting the war came to nothing. Resolutions mentioning the 'international crime' of aggression, such as the draft Treaty for Mutual Assistance and the Geneva Protocol, were never ratified. And the Kellogg-Briand Pact, while renouncing war 'as an instrument of national policy', made no mention of aggression, let alone individual responsibility for it. After 1920, the idea of trying national leaders for starting wars lay dormant in international policy-making circles. Not until the closing stages of the Second World War, with the defeat of the Axis powers within sight, did politicians and jurists return to the problem of the disposal of enemy leaders and the role that courts might play in the process. (2013: 45–46)

The end of the Second World War saw the drafting not only of the London and Tokyo Charters for the two International Military Tribunals but also of the Charter of the United Nations (1945), which builds on those successive efforts to outlaw aggression as a policy option for state-makers. Negotiated and drafted during the Second World War and signed by representatives of fifty of the fifty-one founding members of the UN on 24 October 1945, the UN Charter's preamble opens by proclaiming an organizational intent to "save succeeding generations from the scourge of war, which twice in our lifetime has brought untold sorrow to mankind," foregrounding the primacy given to this particular type of political violence. Indeed, the initiation of international armed conflict, particularly among the world's most militarily powerful states, featured here as the preeminent security concern of the twentieth century. Accordingly, Article 2(4) of the UN Charter states that: "All members shall refrain in their international relations from the threat or use of force against the territorial integrity or political independence of any state, or in any other manner inconsistent with the purposes of the United Nations." In so doing, the UN Charter created a general prohibition on the aggressive use of armed force in international affairs, though debate remains over whether this prohibition was a codification of customary international law as it stood at that time or an appreciable advancement in international law (Grey 2010).

The UN Charter provides for two very important exceptions to that general prohibition on the use of armed force. Often referred to as the self-defense provision, Article 51 states that:

> Nothing in the present Charter shall impair the inherent right of individual or collective self-defence if an armed attack occurs against a Member of the United Nations, until the Security Council has taken measures necessary to maintain international peace and security. Measures taken by Members in the exercise of this right of self-defence shall be immediately reported to the Security Council and shall not in any way affect the authority and responsibility of the Security Council under the present Charter to take at any time such action as it deems necessary in order to maintain or restore international peace and security.

State-makers have relied upon this notion of self-defense as a means of justifying their use of armed force in international affairs. A well-known example of this occurred when US President George W. Bush Jr justified his attack and invasion of Iraq in 2003 as a "preemptive use of military force," prefigured in the US National Security Strategy of 2002, though this justification was not welcomed by all within the international community (see Anghie 2004). Given the widespread acceptance of the general prohibition on the aggressive use of armed force, some state-makers have sought to broaden the definition of self-defense to cloak, quite cynically, certain actions with the legal cover of Article 51 (Sellars 2013).

Activities authorized by the UN Security Council under Chapter VII constitute the other important exception to the general prohibition on armed force in international affairs. Salient here is Article 39. It states that "[t]he Security Council shall determine the existence of any threat to the peace, breach of the peace, or act of aggression and shall make recommendations, or decide what measures shall be taken in accordance with Articles 41 and 42, to maintain international peace and security." Article 42 further states:

> Should the Security Council consider that measures [not involving the use of force] provided for in Article 41 would be inadequate or have proved to be inadequate, it may take such action by air, sea, or land forces as may be necessary to maintain or restore international peace and security. Such action may include demonstrations, blockade, and other operations by air, sea, or land forces of Members of the United Nations.

While not specifically mentioned by the UN Charter, such measures include so-called peacekeeping operations, which range from observer missions monitoring ceasefires agreements among states (UN Emergency Force deployed near the Suez Canal and in the Sinai Peninsula and Gaza between 1956 and 1967, for example, or the UN Observer Group in India and Pakistan deployed in Jammu/Kashmir since 1949) to more complex enforcement missions where the management of the military operation is delegated to a UN member-state, as occurred in Korea between 1950 and 1953, and in Iraq between 1990 and 1991 (Lowe et al. 2008). Other measures include sanction regimes targeting UN member-states that have used armed force in international affairs. Iraq was the target of a UN sanctions regime between 1990 and 1991, as were Ethiopia and Eritrea between 1999 and 2001. The birth of several new states in the immediate aftermath of the dissolution of the Republic of Yugoslavia was accompanied by the aggressive use of armed force, which resulted in sanction regimes targeting Serbia and Montenegro as well as Bosnia and Herzegovina between 1992 and 1996 (Charron 2011).

As a partial and ongoing response to a type of political violence recurring in contemporary world affairs, this field of law is built upon foundations laid by various international treaties, the most significant of which is the Charter of the United Nations. The general prohibition on the aggressive use of armed force in international affairs as expressed in Article 2(4) of the UN Charter prohibited, but did not criminalize, state aggression. At the same time, the UN Charter also provided for state use of armed force in limited circumstances, namely either as self-defense or in support of measures duly authorized by the UN Security Council. Sovereign states are, at once, subject to the UN Charter's provisions relating to this prohibition and the objects of that prohibition, though protected here too is the state-based system and, within that system, the peaceful relations among states. While all UN member-states—now some 193 sovereign states—are bound by relevant duties and responsibilities, the five permanent members of the Security Council, each welding the power of veto, can, if they so choose, exempt themselves from the enforcement of that prohibition. The existence of that veto signals the exterior configurations of power which inform and shape this field of law. The provisions for that veto power were drafted by representatives of the United States, United Kingdom, Soviet Union and China, as the victors of the Second World War, and were then presented to delegates at the 1945 San Francisco Conference in the terms of an ultimatum; either accept the veto or be excluded from the treaty. As Danilo Zolo notes, "[t]he pursuit of power on the part of the United States, Britain and the Soviet Union predominated over the sovereignty of all the other nations, and any allusions to peoples, nations or ethnic groups with no political representation at the conference were simply ignored" (2009: 14; see also Simpson 2004).

International Humanitarian Law

Whereas the prohibition on the aggressive use of armed force in international affairs concerns state conduct viz-*a*-viz armed attacks on other sovereign states and seeks to outlaw war's initiation, international humanitarian law concerns the conduct of hostilities once they have commenced and seeks to refrain war's fury. While the former determines when state use of armed force is permissible, the latter determines what type of force is permissible during armed conflict and in what circumstances. This means the field of international humanitarian law has no substantive interest in the lawfulness, or otherwise, of the use of armed force that may have initiated the armed conflict in question. Hence, even those belligerents whose state may have contravened the prohibition on aggressive force, but who are captured during hostilities, are nevertheless entitled to receive the protections granted to them as prisoners of war.

International humanitarian law permits acts of intentional killing and the deliberate injuring of others, which are usually prohibited under domestic law as crimes of murder and grievous assault, respectively. According to the principle of military necessity, certain acts involving armed force needed to defeat an enemy are permissible, though this does not encompass prohibited acts, such as torture (Sanders 2018). Other principles animate this field of law as it seeks to regulate the conduct of armed conflict. One such principle concerns distinction. This principle means that all persons directly engaged in hostilities must always distinguish between combatants and civilians as well as between military objectives and civilian objects. International humanitarian law does, however, tolerate some harm to civilians and some damage to civilian objects in situations of armed conflict. The acceptance of some collateral damage speaks to the principle of proportionality (Turns 2010), though the use of armed force must be appropriate to the military objective sought. Military commanders must take the principles of necessity, distinction and proportion into consideration during their conduct of hostilities and, as such, these principles are part of the basis upon which their actions are potentially judged.

Drawing on these principles, the field of international humanitarian law is sometimes sub-divided into two more specialized areas. The first specialized area, sometimes colloquially called Hague law, concerns warfare's means and methods. It seeks to place certain restrictions on the tactics of armed conflict and to curtail the use of weapons designed to cause their intended victims excessive suffering. Exploding (or dumdum) bullets, poisonous and asphyxiating gases, chemical and biological weapons and, more recently, anti-personnel landmines are some of the better-known tools of violence that have been outlawed (Monin and Gallimore 2002). Significantly, nuclear weapons are now the object of a ban treaty too. The basis of these prohibitions lies in the inability of these weapons to distinguish between combatants and civilians. So-called Geneva law, the second specialized area, seeks to protect those individuals who are *hors de combat* (outside the fight); that is, those victims of armed conflict who, while not actively participating in hostilities, are impacted by the conflict, including ex-combatants, non-combatants, shipwrecked persons, prisoners of war and civilians. Civilians are defined, more-or-less, as anyone not engaged in hostilities, though this has not always been easy for belligerents to determine (Crawford 2015).

While international humanitarian law is derived from various sources, treaties are especially salient in this field. Law that prohibits certain weapons of war draw on The Hague Conventions of 1899 and 1906, as well as on various other treaties.[3] Law protecting certain categories of persons has formed around many treaties, including, the Geneva Conventions of 1864, of 1949 and the supplementary Protocols of 1977. There are, however, almost sixty multilateral treaties that help express international humanitarian law (Turns 2010). Significantly, many of these treaties are products of conference diplomacy and:

> [a]s the law of armed conflict developed throughout the later nineteenth century, and throughout the twentieth century, States (for the most part) repeatedly embraced and affirmed the cardinal principle of distinction in the treaty law and in practice. When confronted with widespread or systemic civilian participation in armed conflict, States responded by developing and revising the law to extend combatant privileges and immunities. (Crawford 2015: 233)

The nomenclature used to refer to this law also matters. While this chapter reflects the growing trend in recent scholarship that refers to these principles and body of rules as international humanitarian law, which places the dictates of humanity in the foreground, military practitioners tend to refer to the same principles and rules as the law of armed conflict, shifting focus away from those in harm's way and the furies associated with this type of political violence. The diverging nomenclature signals that the development of this field of law through conference diplomacy has been led by state-makers and representatives of their militaries.

The scope of international humanitarian law has expanded from armed conflicts fought between and among sovereign states to include armed conflicts that take place within a state's borders. The broadening of this focus is signaled by the agreement on Common Article 3 of the Geneva Conventions (1949), Additional Protocol II (1977) as well as the case law from the ad-hoc criminal tribunal for the former Yugoslavia. This broadening of the scope of international humanitarian law raises important questions about who, exactly, is subject to these laws and who, therefore, has a duty to comply with that law's relevant provisions. Largely negotiated through conference diplomacy, the field comprises a set of state rights and responsibilities relating to the use of armed force by state-authorized combatants. Yet armed non-state groups, who were not involved or represented in the forums drafting and negotiating the major instruments of international humanitarian law, are (at least seemingly) occasionally abiding by these rules and, in some circumstances, enforcing these rules through their own military or criminal courts. While some armed non-state groups have established and operated courts in ways that are consistent with international humanitarian (and human rights law), the question about whether the wider international community should engage with these actors, and how it should do so, remains an open one (Willms 2015). Of course, not all armed non-state groups seek to abide by the international rule of law or endorse the configurations of power that sustain the politics of contemporary world affairs, as some seek to draw international attention to their cause (Hoffman 2006) or revise the foundations of international life as it is experienced today.

Unlike the general prohibition on the aggressive use of armed force in international affairs, which is, to a large extent, a field populated exclusively by states, non-state actors play a particularly important role in the emergence and evolution of the field of international humanitarian law. The most significant nongovernment organization is, of course, the International Committee of the Red Cross (ICRC), established in 1863 after one of its founding members, Henri Dunant, came across a recently concluded battle and witnessed, first hand, the unmediated horrors of warfare, with the dead and wounded left strewn on the battlefield (Dunant 1939). The ICRC sits atop a broader movement that it founded, which has nearly 200 national societies and almost 100 million members worldwide. It has been awarded the Nobel Peace Prize four times; in 1901, 1917, 1944 and 1963. As David P. Forsythe explains, the ICRC:

> ... is an organization that is primarily private but with public dimensions. It manifests liberal ends but conservative means, championing the worth of the individual but proceeding cautiously on the basis of state consent—which can be slow in manifesting itself. It professes to be non-political but is inherently part of humanitarian politics. It promotes international humanitarian law but resorts to public legal judgements mostly as a last resort, preferring to emphasise pragmatic—if principled—service. It is a product of, and is generally sustained by, western (Judeo-Christian) values, but presents itself as a secular and global Good Samaritan. It is part of an international network officially devoted to universal humanitarianism, but one characterized by strong nationalism, including in the past Swiss nationalism. It emphasizes a limited mandate but over time has expanded its activities broadly. (2005: 281)

The ICRC played, and continues to play, important roles in responding to armed conflict as well as other types of political violence. Under the Geneva Conventions of 1949, it has a specific mandate to visit prisoners of war captured during international armed conflict and a right to humanitarian initiative in situations of civil war. The ICRC also helps build respect for international humanitarian law by assisting those who have legal responsibilities, particularly under the Geneva Conventions of 1949, with drafting and passing domestic legislation, training military professionals and promoting understanding of international humanitarian law through universities and other educational institutions. It also reaches out to armed non-state groups and other weapons-bearing actors to promote the values protected by this law.

As a partial response to the seemingly ubiquitous problem of armed conflict in contemporary world affairs, the field of international humanitarian law permits acts of intentional killing and deliberate injury, which are usually prohibited and criminalized in domestic law during times of peace, though the field also places important limits on the use of certain types of weapons and provides for the protection of certain categories of persons who, for no fault of their own, find themselves in harm's way. This field is built upon ground prepared by treaties and custom; the Geneva Conventions of 1949 are so widely accepted that its contents are now considered by most legal scholars and practitioners to form customary law. While states negotiate treaties with one another horizontally, they administer and enforce the provisions of these instruments vertically, that is, within their, respectively, sovereign jurisdictions. While states are key actors within this field, armed non-state groups operating beyond state control can and do act in accordance with the provisions of international humanitarian law, at times looking to enforce the law among its ranks where particular rules are breached. Moreover, the protections offered to civilians show there is more at stake here than the prerogatives of state sovereigns and their combat forces, as does the advocacy and monitoring role played by the ICRC as the guardian of international humanitarian law. The field of international humanitarian law, which coheres around efforts to curtail war's fury, has a more diverse set of actors than that which populate the closely related field prohibiting state aggression.

International Criminal Law

Like the general prohibition on the aggressive use of armed force in international affairs, the field of international criminal law emerged in the immediate aftermath of the Second World War. While the prohibition of mass atrocity has evolved since the nineteenth century, this field has developed significantly through the drafting of various charters and statutes that established international criminal tribunals and courts, and through prosecuting those who commit atrocities from the mid-twentieth century onwards.[4] The first two institutions designed specifically to enforce international criminal law were created through an agreement reached among the victors of the Second World War. Those prosecuted for their atrocities at the Nuremberg and Tokyo trials were nationals of the vanquished states, Germany and Japan, and who held positions of authority and influence within those countries. Fifty years later, the UN Security Council established, in relatively quick succession, a pair of ad-hoc criminal tribunals to prosecute atrocities committed during Yugoslavia's wars of dissolution and Rwanda's civil war, respectively.[5] In 1998, a diplomatic conference held in Rome produced the Rome Statute of the International

Criminal Court, which entered in force in 2002. Unlike its predecessors, the ICC does not prosecute cases in retrospect; that is, the court only considers cases that fall within its temporal jurisdiction, and this can depend on when a state became party to the Rome Statute. Significant here too is the important role played by civil society organizations in the drafting of the Rome Statute during the diplomatic conference, signaling a more inclusive approach to making public international law (Struett 2008).

The treaties establishing the abovementioned tribunals codified substantive crimes; namely, war crimes, crimes against humanity and the crime of genocide. A war crime is an act, including an act by omission, which violates international humanitarian law. To be a war crime, however, an act needs to be a serious violation of international humanitarian law by breaching a rule that protects important values, where that rule is part of an applicable treaty or forms part of customary law, where that breach poses grave consequences for the victim and where the breach necessitates the individual criminal responsibility of the person causing the breach. These acts are criminal not only where they appear as prohibited acts within governments' military manuals and acts of legislation but also where criminal and military courts try them as serious breaches of international humanitarian law. Significantly, a link to an underlying situation of international or internal armed conflict must also exist for an act to be considered a war crime as it is "the insecure and volatile situation of armed conflict that warrants international interest and gives rise to international jurisdiction over the crime" (Cryer et al. 2010: 275). This was not always the case, however, as war crimes were once thought to occur only in situations of international armed conflict and not during armed conflict occurring exclusively within the jurisdiction of a state, which the late Antonio Cassese described as "a glaring and preposterous disparity" (2008: 88).

War crimes tend to exclude crimes committed by a government against its own citizens. Filling this gap, a crime against humanity is an inhumane or odious act, including an act by omission, which is committed within the context of a widespread and systemic attack against a civilian population with knowledge of that attack. For the purposes of this crime, "widespread" generally refers to the cumulative effects of numerous inhumane acts (though it can occur in a single act) and "systemic" generally means a high degree of organization, evident in certain patterns, ongoing acts, as well as the planning and use of significant resources in search of some political ends. The act must be committed, knowingly, as part of an attack against a civilian population, though here knowledge of an attack does not need to be consenting to the motive behind that attack. If the acts of murder, extermination and torture are isolated acts, then these acts fall short of the threshold needed to become a crime against humanity. Although war crimes have been codified in various conventions with more-or-less agreed definitions, crimes against humanity feature in various instruments with contending definitions. Unlike war crimes, crimes against humanity do not require a link to an underlying situation of armed conflict. While the International Military Tribunal sought to connect the "evil in war" to the "evil of war" by considering only those crimes against humanity that took place during the Second World War, there is no longer a need to link this crime with armed conflict. Some scholars suggest that this nexus, enshrined in the London Charter, was a limitation of its jurisdiction, rather than reflecting the state of custom at that time. Schabas (2012) suggests that crimes against humanity served as a means of punishing crimes which were either authorized under Nazi law or tolerated by those in power but also that those who drafted the London Charter probably never considered the possibility that these crimes might someday apply to non-state actors.

Whereas the notion of a crime against humanity existed in the public imagination prior to the Second World War, the crime of genocide emerged during the war and took hold in its immediate aftermath. Ever since Raphael Lemkin coined the term in 1943 to name "a crime without a name," the definition of genocide has been much-contested. By combing "geno-" (the ancient Greek word for race or tribe) and "-cide" (the Latin word for killing) in a way that resembled the formulation of words such as tyranicide, homicide and infanticide, Lemkin coined a short but chilling term that could disturb audiences more than the earlier term of "crimes of barbarity and vandalism." After its appearance in Lemkin's book, entitled *Axis Rule in Occupied Europe* (1944), genocide took hold of people's imagination. It was used by the US delegation at the London Conference, featured in the Nuremberg indictment, was referred to by the international prosecutors at several points during that trial and was mentioned in the final judgment (Cooper 2008). However, common usage and the social sciences now offer overlapping and, at times, contending definitions of it. Despite the Holocaust taking place before and during the Second World War, genocide did not feature as a category of crime in either the London or Tokyo Charters. At that time, genocide was considered a type of crime against humanity, meaning that prior to the Holocaust no juridical authority existed over the crime of genocide.

Acts constituting the crime of genocide were first enunciated in Article 2 of the Convention on the Prevention and Punishment of the Crime of Genocide (1948) and have remained largely unchanged since then. These are as follows: killing members of the group; causing serious bodily or mental harm to members of the group; deliberately inflicting on the group conditions of life calculated to bring about its physical destruction in whole or in part; imposing measures intended to prevent births within this group and forcibly transferring children of that group to another group. Unlike war crimes but like crimes against humanity, the crime of genocide can occur irrespective of any underlying situation of armed conflict. Genocide's *mens rea* element lies in those acts being committed with the intent to destroy, in whole or in part, national, ethnical, racial or religious groups. It is the link between discrimination and destruction that renders the crime of genocide unique among the most serious international crimes, combining "the dangers of collective action with the intent to cause collective destruction on a discriminatory basis" (Danner 2001). Given its explicit intent to destroy another group and the need for collective action in order to realize that intent, genocide is, as a category of serious international crime, perhaps more harmful than either crimes against humanity or war crimes.

While the general prohibition on the aggressive use of armed force in international affairs has its origins in the Covenant of the League of Nations and the General Treaty for the Renunciation of War, and is codified in the London and Tokyo Charters as well as in the UN Charter, it also played a prominent role in international criminal law's evolution in the long aftermath of the Second World War. That general prohibition shaped the crime of aggression as a category of serious international crime in the Rome Statute, though consensus on its codification has only recently been reached on the particular acts and/or omissions constituting the crime. A Review Conference, held at Kampala, Uganda, between 31 May and 11 June 2010, amended the Rome Statute and its ancillary Elements of Crimes to provide the following definition: a crime of aggression "means the planning, preparation, initiation or execution, by a person in a position effectively to exercise control over or to direct the political or military action of a State, of an act of aggression which, by its character, gravity and scale, constitute a manifest violation of the

Charter of the United Nations."[6] The ICC gained jurisdiction over the crime of aggression on 17 July 2018.

The instruments establishing institutions for enforcing international criminal law not only codified substantive crimes—namely, war crimes, crimes against humanity, and the crime of genocide, which often target people based on their affiliation to a group—but also enabled the prosecution of those individuals who committed prohibited acts. In fact, the judgment delivered at Nuremberg declared that "[c]rimes against international law are committed by men, not be abstract entities, and only by punishing individuals who commit such crimes can the provisions of international law be enforced" (International Military Tribunal 1947). According to Slye and Van Schaack (2009: 269) shifting criminal responsibility from the collective group to an individual person constituted a "doctrinal revolution" so entrenched that it is now "far easier to hold individuals responsible for international crimes than states or other collectivities" Yet, for Gerry Simpson, the doctrine of individual responsibility lies in perpetual tension with holding states' accountable for atrocity-related crimes. He argues that:

> The enhanced status and moral appeal of individual criminal responsibility is undermined by the temptations of collective responsibility. It may be that the tension between state crime and individual responsibility (exemplified by the fact that on 26 February 2006 in The Hague, two cases were being heard simultaneously: one, *Prosecutor v. Milosevic*, concerning *individual* responsibility of the former Serb leader, the other, *Bosnia v. Serbia*, also about genocide but this time *state* responsibility for the crime of genocide) cannot be resolved because the structure of international society and the suppositions of our own belief-systems rests upon that tension. (2007: 66)

The ICC is a court of last resort. It was not designed to prosecute every individual suspected of perpetrating serious international crimes. Rather, its mandate is to investigate and then try those individuals who bear the most responsibility for the gravest of these offenses. The ICC sits at the center of the field of international criminal law, which is underpinned by the principle of complementarity that places the onus on domestic legal regimes to prosecute and try those who commit war crimes, crimes against humanity and crimes of genocide. The field of international criminal law is thus something of a nexus between public international law, with its horizontal focus on regulating the conduct of states (and state-makers) within the society of states, and domestic criminal law, with its vertical focus on regulating the conduct of individuals within particular jurisdictions. Furthermore, the universality of these serious international crimes means that they can be tried in courts that are not necessarily in the jurisdiction where the crimes were committed. Its doctrine of individual responsibility and its protection of civilian populations and social groups defined by various collectively shared identity markers means the field of international criminal law differs appreciably from the cognate field of law concerned with prohibiting state aggression. Unlike the two other fields of law so far considered in this chapter, international criminal law does not provide a framework for permitting the use of armed force by states or their authorized agents.[7]

Transnational Criminal Law

The field of transnational criminal law is concerned with suppressing certain criminal activities that either: (i) take place in more than one state; (ii) are committed in one state, but a substantial part of its preparation, planning, direction or control takes places in another; (iii) are committed in one state but involve an organized criminal group that engages in criminal activities in more than one state or (iv) are committed in one state but has substantial effects in another state (Boister 2012). While transnational crime encompasses a broad ambit, it includes uses of armed force that are prohibited and criminalized under the domestic jurisdiction of states. I focus briefly here on only two types of political violence that are of international concern: terrorism and arms trafficking.

There is no authoritative, comprehensive definition for the crime of terrorism in treaty law, signaling that the international response to the phenomenon of terrorism differs sharply from the international response to state aggression, the conduct of armed conflict and the commission of mass atrocity. Antonio Cassese (2008) argued, however, that international terrorism is regulated by international law, notwithstanding these definitional uncertainties. More specifically, Cassese suggested that acts of international terrorism—which are perpetrated during times of peace—are usually already prohibited and criminalized in domestic law, are transnational in character, are conducted to coerce a state or international organization by spreading intense fear among civilians or harming public figures and organizations. Such acts are motivated by political objectives, rather than the hope of personal gain. Cassese went further by suggesting that acts of international terrorism perpetrated during times of peace may also resemble crimes against humanity if the act, already prohibited and criminalized as murder, torture, rape or enforced disappearance among others, formed part of a widespread or systematic attack against civilians. Cassese also suggested that acts of international terrorism—which were perpetrated during situations of armed conflict—are prohibited and criminalized if those acts involve the use of armed force, including the threat of such force, targeted at civilians or *hors de combat* and is intended to spread intense fear among the civilian population (Cassese 2008).

Certain acts relating to the phenomenon of terrorism are covered by various treaties that deal with terrorism thematically.[8] Important here too are counter-terrorism agreements negotiated through various regional intergovernmental organizations.[9] In addition to customary international law, and these thematic and regional treaties, the UN Security Council has also issued resolutions focusing on the suppression of terrorism, such as Resolutions 731 (1992) and 748 (1992) concerning Libya's suspected involvement in the Lockerbie bombing, and Resolutions 1044 (1966) and 1054 (1966) concerning Sudan's protection of persons suspected of attempting to assassinate President Nasser of Egypt, and resolutions 1267 (1999) and 1333 (2000) concerning the Taliban's protection of Osama Bin Laden. The Security Council has authorized resolutions that deal with terrorism more generally, particularly 1368 (2001) and 1373 (2001), both of which reflect the international concern following in the immediate aftermath of the 9/11 attacks on the United States (see also Martini 2021). As Cryer et al. note, however, the Security Council has been the subject of criticism that it has become an unelected world legislature (2010).

Like terrorism, arms trafficking is unlawful in many domestic jurisdictions and is the object of certain treaties. The United Nations Convention against Transnational Organized Crime (2000), including the Protocol against the Illicit Manufacturing of and Trafficking in Firearms, Their Parts and Components and Ammunition (2001), is one such instrument of transnational criminal law. Arms trafficking is prohibited and criminalized in accordance with Article 5 of the Firearms Protocol:

1. Each State Party shall adopt such legislative and other measures as may be necessary to establish as criminal offences the following conduct, when committed intentionally: (a) Illicit manufacturing of

firearms, their parts and components and ammunition; (b) Illicit trafficking in firearms, their parts and components and ammunition; (c) Falsifying or illicitly obliterating, removing or altering the marking(s) on firearms required by article 8 of this Protocol.

2. Each State Party shall also adopt such legislative and other measures as may be necessary to establish as criminal offences the following conduct: (a) Subject to the basic concepts of its legal system, attempting to commit or participating as an accomplice in an offence established in accordance with paragraph 1 of this article; and (b) Organizing, directing, aiding, abetting, facilitating or counselling the commission of an offence established in accordance with paragraph 1 of this article.

These so-called suppression treaties do not, in and of themselves, prohibit and criminalize certain types of political violence. Rather these instruments of international law recognize crimes that already exist within domestic jurisdictions, creating a new set of rights and obligations among the state signatories to cooperate on such matters as information exchange, expert exchange and extradition. As such, these instruments of international law do not authorize new, or place limits on existing, use of armed force by states and state agents in countering terrorism or arms trafficking.

Just as states are both the objects and subjects of the general prohibition on state aggression, transnational criminal law creates obligations for states which frame the field and, if representatives of the state or their agents contravene the provisions of a suppression treaty, then that individual commits an offense as the state breaches its own obligations. Like international humanitarian and international criminal law, the individuals committing transnational crimes are the objects, rather than the subjects, of the obligations owed under a suppression treaty. Like the horizontal and vertical dimensions of international humanitarian law, transnational criminal law comprises treaty obligations between or among states and obligations to apply criminal law to individuals within their jurisdiction. Even though transnational criminal law resembles international criminal law as it too is a field of criminal law which has an international dimension, it differs because, unlike the most serious international crimes, transnational crimes are prohibited and criminalized first under domestic law. Whereas the notion of complementarity, which circulates within the field of international criminal law, produces effects on domestic jurisdictions, serious crimes in common among domestic jurisdictions, which circulate within the field of transnational criminal, law produce comparable effects on the international space (Boister 2012).

Finally, the field of transnational criminal law has roots reaching back to the early modern practices of piracy. Aside from restraining the excesses associated with armed conflict, these practices were among the first transnational crimes to emerge as states began to intentionally coordinate their collective efforts to prohibit, criminalize and prosecute private actors seeking commercial gain while operating largely beyond the limits of state jurisdiction. The concerns of this field are far broader than the types of political violence that states direct at one another, encompassing nefarious activities that are deemed sufficiently troublesome, or immoral, that they become objects of universal jurisdiction (Slye and Van Schaack 2009: 9). Yet while piracy was a pre-modern international crime, it appears to have lost that status during the long Westphalian peace to the extent that it is no longer considered a core international crime (Boister 2012). Schabas, for example, eschews attempts to include piracy within the field of international criminal law because the practices lacks "terrible horror or shock associated with its commission" (2012: 29) and Simpson argues that pirates are not the enemies of mankind, but are, rather, the enemies of empires, including those "particular political projects often masquerading as the 'international community'" (2007: 161).

Contesting the Political Violence of Law

The abovementioned fields of law prohibit and criminalize state aggression, the use of armed force in situations of armed conflict that is disproportionate to the military objective sought or that fails to distinguish between combatants and civilians, crimes against humanity, genocide, and enable cooperation over the suppression of transnational terrorism and arms trafficking. At the same time, these fields also permit certain uses of armed force by states and state agents, though there are important limits to the use of such force. The efficacy of these laws is, however, to be put into question by the persistence of political violence in contemporary world affairs. Despite the widespread acceptance of the general prohibition on state aggression, for instance, states continue to use force in contemporary world affairs. Since the UN Charter was signed in 1945, there have been, moreover, over one hundred armed conflicts claiming over twenty million casualties (Grey 2010). The Genocide Convention of

1948 and the Convention against Torture and Other Cruel, Inhumane or Degrading Treatment or Punishment (1984) have, for example, not so much prevented acts of political violence as they have helped construct categories rendering certain forceful practices as illegitimate and of international concern. Having explored those interrelated fields of law that have emerged, at least in part, as responses to various types of political violence in contemporary world affairs, I now give focus to the key struggles occurring within these social fields.

First and foremost, struggles occur among state-makers as they draft and negotiate various instruments of international law. While the diplomacy focused on the UN Charter of 1945 constitutes high politics among states, it also reveals the power differential between great powers and all other states (Simpson 2004). The diplomatic negotiation of the Geneva Conventions of 1949 reveals struggles between representatives of the military over civilian powers while signaling, too, the ICRC's role as international humanitarian law's guardian. The Rome Statute of 1998 reveals an even broader array of actors, including nongovernmental organizations, involved in the drafting and negotiating processes, though states retain primary as the law's subjects. As the pool of actors involved in the negotiation of these laws expand, there is a very strong sense that these fields are increasingly transnational, rather than either national or international.

Secondly, these horizontal struggles among state-makers concern the objects of the laws of political violence. While the general prohibition on the use of armed force in international affairs concerns aggression by states and their militaries, the field of international humanitarian law is broader, involving combats authorized by the state as well as armed non-state groups. The field of international humanitarian law also recognized categories of protected persons, namely civilians and those former combatants who are no longer engaged in hostilities. As a field, international criminal law takes aim at the individuals responsible for mass atrocity while certain groups are protected by virtue of their collective national, ethnic, racial or religious identities. Transnational criminal law is a field concerned with the cross-border activities of organized crime groups. These objects, which lie at the heart of these interconnecting fields of law, undermine the state's assertion of ontological primacy in the conduct of contemporary world affairs.

Thirdly, struggles also occur over the implementation, administration and enforcement of duties associated with those instruments of international law by state parties and, in some instances, by armed non-state groups. Some states may not possess the capability to enforce their own military and criminal law vertically; that is, within their own jurisdictions. Others might lack the political will, particularly if their own high-ranking nationals are implicated, or resources needed to fulfill their international commitments. One reason for the persistent use of armed force in international affairs could be the lack of corresponding penalties for states and, moreover, an absolute authority determining who can impose such penalties. The monitoring of state compliance relating to any duties and responsibilities flowing from those instruments of law is supported by nongovernmental organizations, particularly the International Committee of the Red Cross, though it tends to communicate its concerns directly to the state under examination. Struggles within these fields can also relate to selectivity of enforcement practices, including self-granted exemptions by any of the five permanent members of the UN Security Council, for instance. The Security Council can also request the Prosecutor of the ICC to defer an investigation for up to twelve months at a time while it maintains the authority to refer situations to the Prosecutor for his or her preliminary investigation, which occurred in the situation of Libya and Sudan, two so-called outlaw states. State parties to the Rome Statute have also referred situations within their respective jurisdictions to the ICC Prosecutor in the expectation, or hope, that the leaders of armed non-state groups will be indicted and, thereby, curtailing those rebels' aspirations to foster greater levels of international legitimacy (Rogers 2018). The US, of course, refuses to recognize the ICC, a policy posture based on a view of American exceptionalism but dressed up in the unrealistic fears of a runaway prosecutor intend on humiliating US forces engaged abroad.

Finally, while laws of political violence can permit, and then limit, the use of armed force by state and state agents, the law itself can also become weaponized as a form of "lawfare." In other words, laws of political violence can be used for purposes other than those which were originally declared. As Orde Kittrie explains, the rise of "lawfare" was contingent on various factors, the most important of which included "the increased number and reach of international laws and tribunals, the rise of nongovernmental organizations focused on law of armed conflict and related issues, the information revolution, and the advance of globalization and thus economic interdependence" (2016: 1). Allegations of lawfare have been at the forefront of criticism directed at the United States and its War on Terror in both its counter-insurgency and anti-terror campaigns. In fact, while transnational terrorism is prohibited and criminalized in most if not all jurisdictions, acts of terrorism have been used to justify state aggression, as an act of self-defence, and the waging of armed conflict. The anti-terrorism policy of the United States in particular, but also those policies pursued by many other democratic and authoritarian regimes, cut across internationally recognized human rights, some of which are supposedly *jus cogens* rights. In other words, powerful states can authorize their own use of armed force, though the limits of such force are opaque when a terrorist act is deemed to be an existential threat to the political community. For the anti-terror operator, constraints on force use become elastic where a permissive legal culture encourages an "anything goes" attitude in times of emergency, though such emergencies no longer seem meaningfully bounded by place or time.

Conclusion

The conduct of contemporary world affairs continues to be shaped in discernible ways by political violence. As Carl Schmitt put it, "the history of international law is a history of the concept of war. International law is, after all, a 'right of war and peace,' *jus belli ac pacis*, and will remain such as long as it remains a law between independent peoples organized as states—so long, in other words, as war is a war between states and not an international civil war" (1937, p. 31). These world affairs are not, however, animated only by the rule of tooth and claw. The rule of law features prominently in state-based responses to an array of contemporary security problems, especially those involving armed force. While acts related to such violence are prohibited and criminalized by laws, states' ability to use, or authorize the use of, armed force is also fettered by some of these laws. Yet these laws of political violence do not erupt into geographical and temporal existence, as though they were some Big Bang of a nascent legal world order. Like the political violence they seek to control, these laws are human-made. These laws are artifacts produced by social fields in the sense meant by Pierre Bourdieu and the followers of his work. As this chapter shows, these social fields are sites of intense contestation, and the instruments of international law that place limits on political violence are vulnerable to becoming a misused as means of achieving other substantive ends.

According to Ruti Teitel (2011), these recent developments in international law signal a profound, though not always recognized, shift away from defending state sovereignty toward protecting human rights enjoyed by persons and peoples. It is a transformation that she describes as the rise of humanity law, "a framework that spans the law of war, international human rights law, and international criminal justice" (4). Teitel sees law's ambit as expanding to counter the growing scope and intensity of political violence, explaining that:

> The humanity law framework provides a normative basis for extending the regulation of violence beyond the traditional scope and categories of law as it evolved in the nineteenth and twentieth centuries; many of the violent conflicts that engage the concern of the world community today are not in the first instance or even at all interstate wars, waged by state actors such as uniformed soldiers. Given the gaps in human protection left often by the laws of war, and its limited applicability to many of these conflicts and many of the relevant actors, the humanity law framework draws on human rights law and conceptions of transnational and international criminal justice, truly to globalize the regulation of violence and, in principle, to protect all those who are vulnerable in situations of armed conflict [...] and to civilians in peacetime. (105–106)

Teitel's views have profound implications for the politics of war as well as the politics of law, as the protections of human rights are no longer tied to a person's or groups' affiliation to a state or like polity. This offers a new way of conceptualizing and practicing human rights protection that is grounded in an international rule of law put in the service of all members of the human species, perhaps paving the way for the birth of a global human society bounded by its common heritage and kindled by its rich diversity.

National legal cultures impose powerful restraints of this global law's potential. As Rebecca Sanders argues:

> The greatest challenge to the substantive realization of human rights and humanitarian rules in this post-9/11 context lies less in the suspension of law than in the incremental revision and erosion of legal norms … . The laws that prohibit torture, arbitrary deprivations of life and liberty, and warrantless surveillance evolved gradually through time. They

> could eventually be undone, not just through the exercise of unmitigated sovereign power, although that remains an omnipresent possibility, but through a quiet and unexceptional process of plausibly legal reinterpretations. Throughout the global war on terror, American policymakers manipulated law to permit what it should constrain. Forging a national security legal culture that resists this logic is necessary if human rights and humanitarian law are to effectively check human rights abuses in the future. (2018: 168)

Despite the fierce doctrinal debates and associated controversies led by legal scholars and practitioners over the laws of political violence, the outcome of the most serious of struggles occurring within these social fields can be determined by configurations of power that are largely exterior to the field. In fact, these fields of law, which concern various types of political violence, are themselves buttressed by the armed force used to sustain a control paradigm that guarantees the security of those who reside comfortably within the world's most powerful states (Rogers 2016). The laws of political violence can, therefore, contribute in important ways to protecting and promotion of internationally recognized human rights, especially in times of war, though it remains to be seen if the underlying configurations of power in world affairs, which animate these fields, will enable the prioritization of the rights of the many ahead of the rights of a select few. That is, of course, part of the trouble with international law.

Notes

1. These laws are often treated as separate systems or branches of public international law by legal scholars and practitioners (See, for instance, Harris and Sivakumran 2015; Boister 2012).
2. Jackson's role was more than prosecutor and he subsequently reflected that "[t]his was the first case I have ever tried when I had first to persuade others that a court should be established, help negotiate its establishment, and when that was done, not only prepare my case but find myself a courtroom in which to try it" (Meltzer 2005: 56).
3. See, for instance: the Protocol for the Prohibition of the Use in War of Asphyxiating, Poisonous or other Gases, and of Bacteriological Methods of Warfare (1925); Convention on the Prohibition of the Development, Production and Stockpiling of Bacteriological

(Biological) and Toxin Weapons and on their Destruction (1972); Convention on Prohibitions or Restrictions on the Use of Certain Conventional Weapons which may be deemed to be Excessively Injurious or to have Indiscriminate Effects (1980); Convention on the Prohibition of the Development, Production, Stockpiling and Use of Chemical Weapons and on their Destruction (1993); Convention on the Prohibition of the Use, Stockpiling, Production and Transfer of Anti-Personnel Mines and on their Destruction (1997); Convention on Cluster Munitions (2008) and the Treaty on the Prohibition of Nuclear Weapons (2017) which is not yet in force but is attracting signatories.

4. Relevant treaties here include: London Agreement of 8 August 1945—with the Charter of the International Military Tribunal in International Military Tribunal Trial of the Major War Criminals before the International Military Tribunal, Nuremberg 14 November 1945–1 October 1946 Nuremberg, Germany; Charter of the International Military Tribunal for the Far East (as amended 26 April 1946); Statute of the International Criminal Tribunal for the Prosecution of Persons Responsible for Serious Violations of International Humanitarian Law Committed in the Territory of the Former Yugoslavia since 1991 (1994); Statute of the International Criminal Tribunal for the Prosecution of Persons Responsible for Genocide and Other Serious Violations of International Humanitarian Law Committed in the Territory of Rwanda and Rwandan Citizens Responsible for Genocide and Other such Violations Committed in the Territory of Neighboring States, between 1 January 1994 and 31 December 1994 (1995); and Rome Statute of the International Criminal Court (1998).
5. It is worth noting that the victors of the Second World War, who were heavily involved in establishing these first international military tribunals—namely, China, France, Russia, the United Kingdom and the United States— became the five permanent members of the Security Council.
6. "Act of aggression" means the use of armed force by a State against the sovereignty, territorial integrity or political independence of another State, or in any other manner inconsistent with the Charter of the United Nations. Any of the following acts, regardless of a declaration of war, shall, in accordance with United Nations General Assembly resolution 3314 (XXIX) of 14 December 1974, qualify as

an act of aggression: (a) The invasion or attack by the armed forces of a State of the territory of another State, or any military occupation, however temporary, resulting from such invasion or attack, or any annexation by the use of force of the territory of another State or part thereof; (b) Bombardment by the armed forces of a State against the territory of another State or the use of any weapons by a State against the territory of another State; (c) The blockade of the ports or coasts of a State by the armed forces of another State; (d) An attack by the armed forces of a State on the land, sea or air forces, or marine and air fleets of another State; (e) The use of armed forces of one State which are within the territory of another State with the agreement of the receiving State, in contravention of the conditions provided for in the agreement or any extension of their presence in such territory beyond the termination of the agreement; (f) The action of a State in allowing its territory, which it has placed at the disposal of another State, to be used by that other State for perpetrating an act of aggression against a third State; (g) The sending by or on behalf of a State of armed bands, groups, irregulars or mercenaries, which carry out acts of armed force against another State of such gravity as to amount to the acts listed above, or its substantial involvement therein.

7. However, representing a radical departure from the highly controversial muscular humanitarian interventions of the 1990s, the logic of the "Responsibility to Protect" (R2P) does. Adopted in September 2005 by the UN General Assembly as part of the UN World Summit's Outcome Document, R2P gained traction during the first decade of the new millennium. It was first used and defined as the title for the 2001 report of the International Commission on Intervention and State Sovereignty (ICISS). R2P also featured in the report of the UN Secretary-General's High-Level Panel on Threats, Challenges, and Change, entitled *A More Secure World: Our Shared Responsibility* (2004). Former UN Secretary-General Kofi Annan embraced R2P in his own report, *In Larger Freedom: Toward Development, Security and Human Rights for All* (2005), and in 2006 the UN Security Council reaffirmed R2P in Resolution 1674. R2P has three interrelated aspects: first, the state has the primary responsibility for protecting its own population from mass atrocity; second, the international community is responsible for assisting states to protect those populations from mass atrocity;

and third, UN member-states are responsible, through the Security Council, for protecting at-risk populations when the host state fails to provide the necessary protection. In addition to recognizing the international community's responsibility to react to atrocities in the making, R2P recognizes the international community's responsibility to help prevent those atrocities from occurring in the first place as well as its responsibility to help rebuild governments, economies, and societies in the aftermath of mass atrocity (Rogers 2010).

8. Cryer et al. (2010) mention eleven such agreements: Convention for the Suppression of Unlawful Seizure of Aircraft (1970); Convention for the Suppression of Unlawful Acts against the Safety of Civil Aviation (1971) and its Protocol for the Suppression of Unlawful Acts of Violence at Airports Serving International Civil Aviation (1988); Convention on the Prevention and Punishment of Crimes Against Internationally Protected Persons, including Diplomatic Persons (1973); International Convention against the Taking of Hostages (1979); Convention on the Physical Protection of Nuclear Material (1980); Convention on the Suppression of Unlawful Acts Against the Safety of Maritime Navigation (1988) and its Protocol for the Suppression of Unlawful Acts against the Safety of Fixed Platforms located on the Continental Shelf (1988); International Convention for the Suppression of Terrorist Bombings (1997); International Convention for the Suppression of the Financing of Terrorism (1999) and International Convention for the Suppression of Acts of Nuclear Terrorism (2005).
9. These include: Arab Convention on the Suppression of Terrorism (1998); Convention of the Organisation of the Islamic Conference on Combating International Terrorism (1999); European Convention on the Suppression of Terrorism (1977); OAS Convention to Prevent and Punish Acts of Terrorism Taking the Form of Crimes against Persons and Related Extortion that are of International Significance (1971); OAU Convention on the Prevention and Combating of Terrorism (1999); South Asian Association for Regional Cooperation on Suppression of Terrorism (1987); Treaty on Cooperation among State Members of the Commonwealth of Independent States in Combating Terrorism (1999) and European Convention on the Prevention of Terrorism (2005).

References

Anghie A (2004) Imperialism, Sovereignty and the Making of International Law. Cambridge University Press, Cambridge.

Boister N (2012) An Introduction to Transnational Criminal Law. Oxford University Press, Oxford.

Bourdieu P (1987) The Force of Law: Toward a Sociology of the Juridical Field. The Hastings Law Journal 38(July): 814–853.

Cassese A (2008) International Criminal Law (2nd ed). Oxford University Press, Oxford.

Charron A (2011) UN Sanctions and Conflict: Responding to Peace and Security Threats. Routledge, New York.

Cooper J (2008) Raphael Lemkin and the Struggle for the Genocide Convention. Palgrave Macmillan, New York.

Crawford E (2015) Identifying the Enemy: Civilian Participation in Armed Conflict. Oxford University Press, Oxford.

Cryer R, Friman H, Robinson D, and Wilmshurst E, eds. (2010) An Introduction to International Criminal Law and Procedure (2nd ed). Cambridge University Press, Cambridge.

Danner AM (2001) Constructing a Hierarchy of Crimes in International Law Sentencing. Virginia Law Review 87(3): 415.

Dunant H (1939) A Memory of Solferino. International Committee of the Red Cross, Geneva, Switzerland.

Forsythe DJ (2005) The Humanitarians: The International Committee of the Red Cross. Cambridge University Press, Cambridge.

Grey C (2010) The Use of Force and the International Legal Order. In International Law, ed. Evans M (4th ed), 618–648. Oxford University Press, Oxford.

Harris D and Sivakumaran S (2015) Cases and Materials on International Law. Thomson Reuters, London.

Hoffman B (2006) Inside Terrorism (revised and expanded ed). Colombia University Press, New York.

Keenan JB (1946) Opening Statement of the Prosecution Northcroft Archive (Prosecution's Document file) Macmillan Brown Library, University of Canterbury, New Zealand.

Kittrie OF (2016) Lawfare: Law as a Weapon of War. Oxford University Press, Oxford.

Lowe V, Roberts A, Welsh J and Zaum D, eds. (2008) The United Nations Security Council and War: The Evolution of Thought and Practice since 1945. Oxford University Press, Oxford.

Martini A (2021) The UN and Counter-Terrorism: Global Hegemonies, Power and Identities. Routledge, New York and London.

Meltzer BD (2005) Robert H Jackson: Nuremberg's Architect and Advocate. Albany Law Review 68: 55.
Monin L and Gallimore A (2002) The Devil's Gardens: A History of Landmines. Pimlico, London.
Rogers D (2018) Law, Politics and the Limits of Prosecuting Mass Atrocity. Palgrave Macmillan, New York.
Rogers P (2016) Irregular War: ISIS and the New Threat from the Margins. I.B. Tauris, London and New York.
Sanders R (2018) Plausible Legality: Legal Culture and Political Imperative in the Global War on Terror. Oxford University Press, Oxford.
Schabas W (2012) Unimaginable Atrocities: Justice, Politics, and Rights at the War Crimes Tribunals. Oxford University Press, Oxford.
Schmitt C (1937) The Turn to the Discriminating Concept of War. In Carl Schmitt Writing on War, ed. and trans. Nunan T. Polity, Cambridge.
Sellars K (2013) 'Crimes Against Peace' and International Law. Cambridge University Press, Cambridge.
Simpson G (2004) Great Powers and Outlaw States: Unequal Sovereigns in the International Legal Order. Cambridge University Press, Cambridge.
Simpson G (2007) Law, War and Crime: War Crime Trials and the Reinvention of International Law. Polity, Cambridge.
Slye RC & Van Schaack B (2009) International Criminal Law. Aspen Publishers, New York
Struett MJ (2008) The Politics of Constructing the International Criminal Court: NGOs, Discourse, and Agency. Palgrave Macmillan, New York
Teitel RG (2011) Humanity's Law. Oxford University Press, Oxford
Terdiman R (1987) Translator's Introduction for 'The Force of Law: Towards a Sociology of the Juridical Field' by Pierre Bourdieu in The Hastings Law Journal 38 (July): 805–813
Thirlway H (2010) The Sources of International Law in Evans M ed. International Law (4th ed) Oxford University Press, Oxford
Turns D (2010) The Law of Armed Conflict (International Humanitarian Law) in Evans M ed. International Law (4th ed) Oxford University Press, Oxford
Willms J (2015) "Courts of armed groups—A tool for inducing higher compliance with international humanitarian law? In Inducing Compliance with International Humanitarian Law: Lessons from the Great Lakes Region, ed Kriger H. Cambridge University Press, Cambridge
Zolo, D (2009) Victors' Justice: From Nuremberg to Baghdad. Verso, London and New York

Instruments of International Law

Arab Convention on the Suppression of Terrorism (1998).
Charter of the United Nations (1945).
Covenant of the League of Nations (1919).
Convention Against Torture and Other Cruel, Inhumane or Degrading Treatment or Punishment (1984).
Convention of the Organisation of the Islamic Conference on Combating International Terrorism (1999).
Convention for the Suppression of Unlawful Seizure of Aircraft (1970).
Convention for the Suppression of Unlawful Acts Against the Safety of Civil Aviation (1971) and Its Protocol for the Suppression of Unlawful Acts of Violence at Airports Serving International Civil Aviation (1988).
Convention on the Suppression of Unlawful Acts Against the Safety of Maritime Navigation (1988) and Its Protocol for the Suppression of Unlawful Acts Against the Safety of Fixed Platforms Located on the Continental Shelf (1988).
Convention on the Physical Protection of Nuclear Material (1980).
Convention on the Prevention and Punishment of Crimes Against Internationally Protected Persons, Including Diplomatic Persons (1973).
Convention on the Prevention and Punishment of the Crime of Genocide (1948).
European Convention on the Suppression of Terrorism (1977).
European Convention on the Prevention of Terrorism (2005).
General Treaty for the Renunciation of War as an Instrument of National Policy (1928).
Geneva Conventions of 1864, of 1949 and the supplementary Protocols of 1977.
International Convention against the Taking of Hostages (1979).
International Convention for the Suppression of Terrorist Bombings (1997).
International Convention for the Suppression of the Financing of Terrorism (1999).
International Convention for the Suppression of Acts of Nuclear Terrorism (2005).
International Military Tribunal (1947) Trial of the Major War Criminals before the International Military Tribunal II Proceedings, 14 November–30 November 1945. Nuremberg, Germany.
OAS Convention to Prevent and Punish Acts of Terrorism Taking the Form of Crimes against Persons and Related Extortion that are of International Significance (1971).
OAU Convention on the Prevention and Combating of Terrorism (1999).
South Asian Association for Regional Cooperation on Suppression of Terrorism (1987).

Treaty on Cooperation among State Members of the Commonwealth of Independent States in Combating Terrorism (1999).
Treaty of Peace Between the Allied and Associated Powers and Germany (1918).
United Nations Convention against Transnational Organized Crime (2000), including the Protocol against the Illicit Manufacturing of and Trafficking in Firearms, Their Parts and Components and Ammunition (2001).

CHAPTER 4

The Tragedy of Human Rights

Abstract The rise of human rights is connected to wars of global significance while the value placed on those emergent rights is recognized in international law, especially the Universal Declaration of Human Rights adopted by the UN General Assembly in 1948. In this penultimate chapter, I situate the promotion and protection of human rights within the modernist project before refocusing my discussion at the scale of the human species during the epoch of the Anthropocene, which is defined in large part by the consequences flowing from humanity's untrammeled and harmful dominion over nature. With an eye to an ever-darkening horizon, I acknowledge that the politico-cultural project of modernity is based on, and sustained by, routines of domination and exploitation, which manifest not only as violence among groups, communities and societies but also as violence used by humans against other non-human species, plant life and the environment more generally. Drawing on Bruno Latour's critique of political ecology, I argue that the tragedy of human rights unfolds as actions, taken in the name of these rights, place humanity in ever greater peril precisely because such actions are driven by an anthropocentric commitment that crowds out regard of, and care for, other life forms and life systems. It is a tragedy, somewhat reminiscent of the tragedy of the commons, not only because the human suffering accompanying the

D. Rogers, *Wars, Laws, Rights and the Making of Global Insecurities*, Human Rights Interventions,
https://doi.org/10.1007/978-3-030-90162-2_4

aggressive use of armed force in the service of these rights is avoidable but also because humanity itself is imperiled by the pursuit of those rights. I end this chapter by pleading for the right to life of non-human species to be taken seriously and more strongly respected in conduct of future world affairs.

Keywords Modernity · Anthropocene · Humanity · Non-human species · Bruno Latour

Human Rights and the Modernist Project

War and Human Rights

Contestation over special rights, such as liberty of religious conscience, contributed to the outbreak of wars of global significance, including Europe's Religious Wars of the seventeenth century. The roots of the Thirty Years War lay in the Protestant Reformation and the deepening division among Christendom. On the one hand, Protestant theology conceptualized individuals as salvation-seeking moral agents with unmediated access to God's will whereas Catholics, on the other hand, embraced the Roman Church and its role mediating the individual's access to God's will. Given their belief that individuals could only obtain salvation through their faith, Protestants valued freedom of religion, but thereby challenged the Catholic Church's transnational authority. Protestant intellectuals were especially important in proclaiming that individuals possessed certain inalienable features that were worth protecting, an idea that resonated among the great rights theorists of the seventeenth century (who were almost always Protestants too) (Reus-Smit 2013).

Contestation over these special rights also featured as part of the Westphalian settlement of 1648 and the subsequent rise and spread of the states-based system in the long aftermath of that Westphalian peace. Some scholars, particularly scholars of disciplinary International Relations, explain the rise of the Westphalian peace as a victory of sovereignty over religion, but that is an oversimplification. As Christian Reus-Smit (2013) has shown, while the Westphalian peace treaties framed the creation of various states endowed with collective rights of sovereignty, this sovereignty was accompanied by the granting of religious freedom to individuals. This afforded religious minorities—Catholics residing in Protestant states for instance—with some protection from persecution. Similarly, populations were no longer required to convert their religion as their sovereign might. Rodley concurs when he writes that "[t]he social contract, by which each individual ceded some of his or her naturally endowed autonomy to ensure the meeting of shared needs, did not require the total surrender of that autonomy. Human rights marked the boundary of the cession. The individual retained some sovereignty too" (2010: 784).

While rival nationalisms and empires helped unleash the twentieth century's two world wars, the individual rights to be enjoyed by all human beings became a key component of the settlement and long peace that followed the Second World War. Indeed, it was only after the Second World War, the deadliest armed conflict in human history to date, had ended that a "zone of application" for these individual rights become large enough to be considered universal. From this time onwards, the "special" individual rights enjoyed by some human beings based on their privileged position become "general" human rights enjoyed by every person on the grounds that each individual counted as a separate moral being (Reus-Smit 2013: 6). In other words, the notion of special rights, say, to religious freedom granted to certain individuals during the religious wars, had transformed over three centuries to encompass general rights concerning civil and political freedoms held by all individuals by virtue of their being human.

Law and Human Rights

These human rights feature in the first article of the Charter of the United Nations, which calls for "international cooperation in … promoting and encouraging respect for human rights and fundamental freedoms for all without distinction as to race, sex, language or religion." Human rights became a matter of international concern the moment the UN Charter entered into force, especially as Articles 55 and 56 oblige states to work independently and collectively in order promote them (Rodley 2010). While the UN Charter offered no details on the meaning of the term human rights and the associated fundamental freedoms, the Universal Declaration of Human Rights (UDHR) did.

While the establishment of the International Labor Organization in 1919 was aimed at helping protect the freedom of association for trade unionists, human rights found expression in instruments of international law as early as the Slavery Convention of 1926, which sought to prevent and suppress the slave trade and to end slavery in all its forms (Rodley 2010). However, the UDHR has become a foundational pillar of the rule of law emerging after the Second World War. Its negotiation was an important step toward internationalizing the doctrine of human rights across the world. International standards, which are sometimes used to name and shame those who violate human rights with some regularity, have emerged from the Declaration's articles, signifying its normative value (Pettman 2010).

Prepared by a team comprising individuals with various legal backgrounds from around the world, the UDHR took just over two years to draft. It was not only, in part, a response to the horrors witnessed during the Second World War but also, in part, a strong opprobrium against the cruelty suffered through mass atrocities, including the Holocaust among other war crimes and crimes against humanity committed in the first half of the twentieth century. Proclaimed by the UN General Assembly in Paris on 10 December 1948 without dissent, the UDHR has found widespread acceptance among the society of states. The national constitutions of over eighty states make explicit reference to it while sixty states afford some kind of authority to it, including twenty-six constitutions that acknowledge that the UDHR supersedes their domestic legal systems in some cases. With only thirty articles, the UDHR is "short and punchy" (Kaplan 2018: 17), though, taken as a whole, the Declaration offers a pluralistic framework for human rights advocates. As Seth Kaplan explains:

> In order to maximize the reach of their creation, the drafters used easy-to-understand language, kept the length short, changed 'international' in the title to 'universal,' and avoided issues that would in any way be controversial. They also put people and their social institutions front and centre, rarely mentioning the state. They understood that ultimately the success of their endeavor depended on inspiring change in how people treated each other—in their relationships—across society. (2018: 24)

The Declaration opens with a preamble comprising seven paragraphs that outline the reasons behind its creation. Its first two articles refer to the Declaration's various principles and core values, which include dignity, liberty, equality and brotherhood. The Declaration's main body provides for four sets of human rights: Articles 3 through to 11 concern the rights held by the individuals; Articles 12 through to 17 speak to the ways in which individuals relate to each other and to groups; Articles 18 through to 21 refer to concerns of spiritual, public and political nature and Articles 22 through to 27 concern economic, social and cultural rights. Articles 28, 29 and 30 close out the UDHR by situating individuals within their wider societal contexts and by pointing to the limits of human rights, the duties and responsibilities that accompany such rights, and sequencing of their realization.[1] While the UDHR articulates a set of human rights, these rights are connected and, in some cases, interrelated. This means the Declaration expresses ideas that need to be balanced against other ideas found in the same document and speaks of certain rights that cannot be understood or protected without regard to other rights. The UDHR is, according to Kaplan, a "body of principles meant to be read as an integrated whole, indivisible, interdependent, and interrelated, with an organic entity" (2018: 39).

Articulating a set of moral claims that any person—by virtue of their humanity—may claim whatever their race, class, gender, age, or spiritual belief, the UDHR offers an abstracted version of a hyper-individual who exists without those secondary identity markers and is, for Pettman, "[t]he most notable example of the discourse of neo-individualism ...." (2010: 132). In an article-by-article analysis of the UDHR, Pettman sees language which clearly expresses a preference for individualism, autonomy and a rationalist, liberal notion of self, as well as a preference for liberal styled-democratic governance. Contrastingly, Kaplan points out that "[t]he Declaration uses the word 'person' to emphasise the social dimension of personhood .... The term 'person' stands in contrast to 'individual'" (2018. 38). While Pettman does acknowledge that Article 15 of the UDHR embraces another form of identity, namely nationalism, he also suggests that this is not in itself a contradiction as individualism concerns the independent self, whereas nationalism concerns the collective (or neo-tribal) self. Pettman concludes, as follows:

> So, a mixed bag overall, but one that generally articulates the politico-social perspective of the individualist. There are articles that revert to nationalism and socialism, and even one that casts forward to collectivism, but in the main the analytic focus is firmly fixed on the moral claims that an autonomous individual might make. The underlying assumptions are that we are rationalistic beings and that our rationalism is best articulated

> in terms of the essential human capacity for calculation. The result is an abstract code of conduct deemed sufficiently context-free to serve as a "common standard ... for all peoples and all nations" and one that can be taught and implemented as such. (2010: 141)

The UDHR has been subjected to criticism on the grounds that, as a byproduct of a particular politico-culture, its content reflects and re-inscribes the rationalist and liberal character of a modernist project emerging out of European Christendom. In other words, the Declaration's pretense toward universalism has been unmasked as a form of cultural relativism projected on to other politico-cultures. As such, the UDHR has prompted the promulgation of alternative understandings of human rights, such as the Universal Islamic Declaration of Human Rights (1981), which perceives every human being as divine, a sacral status embodied with rights protected under religious law (Pettman 2010: 133). However, claims that the UDHR is overly euro-centric might be somewhat exaggerated because its contents offer a view of humanity that reflects concern with social context, institutions and practices that abound in the Global South more than it reflects the secular concern for the individual found in contemporary western societies. This is because the drafting of the document was shaped more by the "dignitarian rights tradition of Latin America and continental Europe than by the more individualistic Anglo-American rights tradition ..." (Kaplan 2018: 19).

The set of human rights put forth in the UDHR also helped to shape postcolonial dimensions of the prevailing world order. Following the end of the Second World War, several anti-colonial movements pointed to the inconsistent way in which Europeans denied their colonial subjects the very civil and political rights which they cherished at home. Casting light on this hypocrisy was an important tactic for delegitimizing the colossal institutions of empire, building on the nexus between the collective right to self-determination and the emerging norm of human rights, especially within the forums of the United Nations where newly independent states sought international recognition. In fact, many postcolonial independence movements were inspired by the desire to have their individual civil and political rights recognized. While some proclaim that international human rights law is largely a western project, postcolonial independence movements were directly involved in negotiating key instruments of international law and where often seeking to apply the norms associated with international human rights in ways that challenged the conduct of major European and other western states (Reus-Smit 2013).

The human rights elaborated within the UDHR also informed the development of international human rights law following the end of the Second World War and, then, during a period that witnessed the birth of many new postcolonial states. While a system of law promising and protecting human rights has roots in the UN Charter, its framing architecture is found in an International Bill of Human Rights, which comprises not only the UDHR, but also the International Covenants on Economic, Social and Cultural Rights (IECSCR) and on Civil and Political Rights (ICCPR), including the (first) Optional Protocol to the ICCPR.[2] There are, of course, a larger corpus of "core" treaties[3] and regional human rights treaties also exist.[4] The International Bill of Human Rights is especially important because it not only framed human rights as an issue of general international law but also created specific obligations and mechanisms for monitoring compliance with those duties. Whereas the UDHR elaborates principles behind a catalog of human rights, these treaties provide more precision to those rights, give them legal force and provide for mechanisms monitoring states' progress toward implementing and observing those treaties' substantive provisions (Rodley 2010).

The distribution of obligations within the system of international human rights law has an obvious horizontal dimension that binds states through their commitment to the rule of public international law. In addition to states recognizing and creating duties to other states, this system also has significant vertical dimensions, whereby international responsibilities reach down into a state's domestic legal regime. In fact, many of the new postcolonial states emerging in the aftermath of the Second World War have constitutional bills of rights that draw heavily on, and further entrench, the understanding of human rights contained in the UDHR. At the intersection of these horizontal and vertical dimensions, states act in accordance with their international obligations by respecting the human rights enjoyed by those individuals found within that state's jurisdiction, and protecting those individuals' human rights from other individuals, groups or states (Rodley 2010).

This system of international human rights law is underscored by various monitoring and enforcement mechanisms. At the apex of these mechanisms sits the Human Rights Council (HRC), now the principal UN human rights organ, which succeeded the somewhat toothless Commission of Human Rights (Rodley 2010). Rather than report to the UN Economic and Social Council, as its predecessor had, the HRC reports to the UN General Assembly and is required to undertake a universal periodic review of all UN member-states' conduct vis-à-vis their human rights responsibilities. Buttressing the HRC's monitoring efforts are various committees. Nine such committees were established in accordance with the abovementioned "core" human rights treaties and a subcommittee on torture was established under the Optional Protocol.[5] Comprising between 10 and 25 members, these committees of subject-matter experts are nominated by their sovereign states but serve in their capacity as individual citizens, usually for four-year terms but they are sometimes re-elected. These committees interpret and apply legal instruments and, generally speaking, their functions include, firstly, reviewing periodic State reports, including state responses to specific written questions put by the committee. Even where a state is overdue in submitting their periodic reports, the committee can still consider the state's human rights situation, though sometimes the committee itself suffers a backlog of reports submitted but not yet considered. Secondly, these committees issue "general comments" consisting of guidance to States outlining a committee's understanding of what State's obligation under the respective treaty may be. These are deemed authoritative interpretations of the treaties, based on extensive experience of reviewing periodic reports and of examining individual cases. Thirdly, these committees receive and consider individual complaints, requesting further information from the parties concerned and, fourthly, can in some cases receive and consider interstate complaints. Taken together, these committees and their functions have created "a substantial network of what are usually called Charter-based human rights procedures" (Rodley 2010: 804).

Beyond the HRC's formal oversight mechanism and the various committees that are creatures of core human rights treaties lies a broader international human rights community comprising representatives of intergovernmental organizations, an array of social movements and nongovernmental organizations, as well as what might be described as peace researchers (see Cortright 2008). Despite their differing roles, disparate voices and disagreements, a consensus underpins this community. Modern westerners holding very strong attachments to the notion of individualism, who are, in global terms, a very small minority, largely determine the possibilities and limitations of the human rights agenda.

Members of this group assume leadership roles in global social movements and nongovernmental organizations, dominate western universities and thereby shape the contours of the relevant pools of scholarship and inform media reporting. Their influence registers beyond the Global North, however, as these modern westerners frame the priorities for resourcing local nongovernmental organizations operating in the Global South. The strength of this ideological commitment closes spaces available for debate, contestation and dissenting views, foreclosing alterative notions of human rights and other possible human rights practices. This, in turn, signals an important, but often unremarked upon, disconnect between the drafters of the UDHR, which appreciated that human rights are understood differently in locations spread across the world, and most contemporary human rights activists, who, as modernists, see human rights as universal, as opposed to pluralistically, and insist that international human rights law commits states to a western liberal notion of those rights (Kaplan 2018).

Humanity and the Anthropocene

Coined by Eugene Stormer in the 1980s before it was introduced into the public imagination by Nobel laureate Paul Crutzen in the early 2000s, the Anthropocene is a conceptual term that refers to a geological epoch marked by humanity's pernicious impact on the planet (Chandler 2018). In other words, the Anthropocene demarcates a period of planetary time when humanity, viewing itself as a life force distinct to, and separate from, nature, and proclaiming and then exercising dominion over the natural world, altered the trajectories of planetary life in discernible ways. This epoch is characterized by the enormous magnitude of humanity's impact on earth's living systems, including its environment, an impact which resembles the most powerful forces of nature. "Humanity," in this sense, has become in and of itself "... a major geological force" (Bonneuil and Fressoz 2016: xii) and "humans are geological agents" (Harrington 2016: 479) whose actions are now writing "the geological record" (482).

The Anthropocene matters because it signals the extent to which humanity has affected seriously and injuriously, and continues to affect seriously and injuriously, the natural world and non-human life forms. According to Bonneuil and Fressoz (2016), these harmful effects register in various ways. Humans have burnt coal and other fossil fuels generating 1,500 billion tons of carbon dioxide, which damages the earth's atmosphere. Emitted by human activity, greenhouse gases, such as methane, nitrous oxide and carbon dioxide, have increased since 1750 by 150, 63 and 43%, respectively, contributing to rising planetary temperatures. The United Nations Intergovernmental Panel on Climate Change forecasts an increase in the earth's temperature of between 2 and 6% by the end of this century, with devastating consequences for the planet's life systems. That estimate is an alarming acceleration given the average 0.8% rise in temperature since the mid-nineteenth century. The planet's rising temperature reduces ice coverage and increases sea levels, an immediate problem for coastal populations and those who live on low-lying islands. Human activity is also the driving force behind the degradation of the world's ecosystems, which includes the extinction of non-human species at a rate that is between 100 and 1000 times greater than in any other period of ecological time; current estimates project one-fifth of all existing species will be extinct within a decade.

Meanwhile, the world's fish stocks continue to be overfished and its oceans polluted. Humans and their domesticated animals use almost all of the available biomass for their own needs and wants, effectively starving some 30,000 land-dwelling vertebrate species. This imploding biosphere—which is no longer capable of effectively pollinating, capturing carbon, protecting from erosion and regulating water quality and quantity to the extent needed to sustain the multitudinous life forms on this planet—is only intensified by the spread of synthetic chemical molecules across the planet's living tissue. Furthermore, the human population has increased from 900 million in 1800 to seven billion in 2012, consuming annually one and a half times what the planet can sustainably produce in a year. The wealthiest 500 million of these 7 billion people "are not only consuming the fruits of the trees on which we sit, but also sawing through its branches" (Bonneuil and Fressoz 2016: 9). Jairus Victor Grove sums up the Anthropocence's impact astutely when he writes: "The global network of open wounds, bruises, and scar tissue that runs over the surface of the planet, through its water table and abandoned mine shafts that sprawl out on the vast ocean floor, exceeds the migratory and circulation patterns of any other species or even family of species. Five hundred years of geopolitics has built a global savage ecology" (2019: 7).

In addition to highlighting the extinction of non-human species, the Anthropocene signals the extent to which humanity seriously harms other life forms for reasons of pleasure, comfort and entertainment, such as horseracing (Boyd 2015). Perhaps the most repugnant form of mistreating animals is to conceive of them as meat, whereby the life-cycle of entire populations of various species becomes the subject of human food production systems. As Daniel Kirjner (2015) points out, the commodification of species life has been driven by industrial techniques and processes which have developed over the last three hundred years. The numbers are, by any reckoning, staggering. Kirjner estimates that, in most large abattoirs, an animal is killed every few seconds, meaning that "hundreds of millions of cattle, pigs, and sheep are raised and slaughtered in the United States alone each year; and for poultry the figure is a staggering three billion" (2015: 138–139).[6] Industrialized forms of animal agriculture continue to play important roles producing and exacerbating other environmental problems, including ongoing and large-scale deforestation, the emission of greenhouse gases, the acceleration of extinction rates of other life forms and the depletion of scarce natural resources. These problems are particularly acute in Brazil where the world's largest commercial herd of cattle, some 65 million animals, takes priority over the life systems supported by Brazil's Amazonian rainforest, of which over three-quarters (403,000 miles) has already been re-purposed for various economic uses. The increasing number of cattle is prompting an unprecedented transformation of Brazil's rainforests, which remains, for the time being at least, one of the world's richest sources of biodiversity. Krijner puts it with chilling clarity when he writes: "The oppression of animals in the Anthropocene is certainly not justified by biological differences between humans and non-humans. Animal exploitation stems from a reframing of life caused by capitalist commodification, by a predatory culture that glorifies male violence, and by the fragmentation and stigmatization of emotion as a lesser form of expression than cold rationality and violent domination" (2015: 146).

The overall effect of humanity's relationship to non-human life on earth, as it is to the life systems of this planet, is nothing short of a looming catastrophe. Bonneuil and Fresnoz's assessment is unequivocal and disturbing:

> The warning given by the Anthropocene concept, and the recent advances in the sciences of the Earth system, thus go much further than an anthropocentric view of the 'environmental crisis,' no matter how alarming. The problem is not only that our environment is being degraded, nor that 'resources' (another category that postulates an external and static character to the Earth and its beings and processes) are being

> exhausted, increasing social inequalities and thus threatening the planet with major geopolitical disturbances. The double reality that the Anthropocene presents is that, on the one hand, the Earth has seen other epochs in the last 4.5 billion years, and life will continue in one form or another with or without humans. But the new states that we are launching the Earth into will bring with them a disorder, penury and violence that will render it less readily habitable by humans. Even if the human species manages to reduce its ecological footprint drastically and invent a more sober civilization, we will not have settled accounts with Gaia. The Earth would take at least centuries if not hundreds of thousands of years to get back to the climatic and geological regime of the Holocene. The traces of our urban, industrial, consumerist, chemical and nuclear age will remain for thousands or even millions of years in the geological archives of the planet. (2015: 21)

This testifies to the fact that the human species is unique in its capability to invent and innovate, not only for its own survival but also to flourish, by adapting to its environment and by manipulating that environment and its multitudinous life forms. This capacity has made humans very successful in terms of the survival of the fittest. Human beings have extracted and exploited nature as a means of increasing its population to the extent that some might describe humanity as a plague on earth which directly and indirectly affects the life chances of all other creatures. Yet implying humanity is a uniform force of nature, the conceptual term of the Anthropocene conceals important divisions among humans, particularly along the lines of sex and gender, race and ethnicity, geography and class and the various inequalities these divisions produce and entrench. In this respect, it is worth acknowledging that the human-made impacts that register during the Anthropocene were made by, and for, a segment of humanity who are often white wealthy males of European heritage (Harrington 2016).

Attempts to trace the Anthropocene's rise pay close attention to the routines of domination and exploitation that animate the modernist project. Bonneuil and Fressoz (2016) suggest that armed force unleashed during the First and Second World Wars (including the use of the atomic bomb) was so shocking that it encouraged critiques of Western modernity and its slew of human, social, ecological and spiritual wreckage. Harrington (2016) uses two markers, both of which are consequences that follow on from political violence, to locate and trace the emergence of the Anthropocene. Firstly, Harrington points to the record dip in atmospheric CO_2 levels that occurred in 1610, a dip which resulted from the violence and disease carried by Europeans as they colonized and annihilated the native inhabitants of the Americas, killing more than 61 million people and thereby prompting a major decline in farming and other agricultural activities. Secondly, Harrington points to the year 1964, when the highest level of radioactivity was recorded following the testing of nuclear bombs. Both dates, Harrington explains "represent the capacity of humans to enact violence, war and destruction. The Anthropocene entangles political, economic, cultural, technological and material processes" (2016: 484). Crutzen places the emergence of the Anthropocene in 1784, with the invention of the steam engine and the Industrial Revolution that followed (Bonneuil and Fressoz 2016: 1). Harrington and Crutzen are not alone in historicizing the Anthropocene's emergence within the modernist project.

Latour's Political Ecology

Bruno Latour signals serious consequences for those who are subject to modernist politics and become, by necessity, experts in surviving conquest, dispossession and annihilation, though he points out that the modernizers are not always immune from their own effects. He pays tribute to ecological movements and green parties that draw attention to the deteriorating condition of ecology within the modernist project, especially since the Industrial Revolution and during the Anthropocene. These social movements and political parties were successful in "transforming everything into vigorous controversies—from beef to the climate, by way of hedges, humid zones, corn, pesticides, diesel fuel, urban planning, and airports—that every material object has taken on its own 'ecological dimension'" (2017: 45). "Thanks to ecology," Latour enthuses, "no development project fails to arouse a protest, no proposition fails to elicit an opposing one .... Ecology has thus succeeded in running politics through its mill by introducing objects that had not previously belonged to the usual preoccupations of public life. It has successfully rescued politics from an overly restrictive definition of the social world. In this sense, political ecology has fully succeeded in changing what is at stake in the public sphere" (2017: 45–46).

Yet Latour also offers a critique of political ecology and its associated practices, questioning the relationship between modernity and nature. He explains that nature is not a separate dimension of reality, but rather, exists as a modernist distinction that totalizes all those non-human living beings sharing a common world, which deliberately reduces political life on this planet to the public life of humanity (2004). Latour wonders why nature was eschewed by political ecologists as something exterior to humanity or as some utile object, rather than considered a partner or ally, and warns that it is easy to become a prisoner of a simplistic concept of nature. Humanity should stop using the word "ecology," he opines, except to refer to a specific scientific field because its current use obscures the interspecies contestations taking place among those inhabiting common dwelling places. He argues further that "[i]f the composition of the air we breathe depends on living beings, the atmosphere is no longer simply the environment in which living beings are located and in which they evolve; it is, in part, a result of their actions. In other words, there are not organisms on one side and an environment on the other, but a coproduction by both" (2017: 76). Insisting that political ecology should be reinvented without the distinction between human and no-human life forms with a progressive understanding of the good common world (2004), Latour goes as far as to suggest that modernity is in a situation of war between those humans who believe they alone exist in the Holocene and those who know they live in the Anthropocene and seek to cohabit with other terrestrials. It is a war, Latour surmises, with civic and moral dimension that divide each of us internally (2017).

Individuals and groups seeking to govern contemporary world affairs tend to securitize a range of political issues, including, of course, irregular migration (Bigo and Tsoukala 2008) and other transnational crimes, such as drugs and firearms trafficking (Williams 2010), but also infectious diseases, such as Human Immuno-deficiency Virus Infection and Acquired Immune Deficiency Syndrome (HIV/AIDS), Severe Acute Respiratory Syndrome (SARS), avian influenza (H5N1) (O'Manique and Fourie 2010) and of course Coronavirus.[7] Some have securitized non-human life, including declaring climate emergencies with respect to widespread environmental degradation. Since 2016, 1770 local governments in 30 countries have declared a climate emergency, in which political leaders recognize that global warming is a serious real-world problem affecting humanity while acknowledging the current approaches to addressing this problem are woefully inadequate (CEDAMIA 2020). The Pope joined the chorus, issuing a declaration in mid-2019, as did the European Union at the end of 2019. In some cases, features of the earth's life systems are represented as a direct threat to political communities, as deadly and as surprising as various types of political violence. As Brian Massumi (2015) points out, in the aftermath of Hurricane Katrina in 2005 President George W. Bush declared weather systems to be like terrorist attacks; violent, unpredictable and irrational.

Describing phenomena found in the natural world as an existential threat to a political community, or even humanity more generally, and having those discursive practices accepted by wider audiences, clears space for further opportunities for humans to exert control over nature. President Bush not only compared the devastation caused by Hurricane Katrina to the destructive force of improvised explosive devices harming American armed forces operating in Iraq but also arrived in New Orleans three weeks later, "land[ing] on the beachhead of natural disaster not as chief executive of the civilian bureaucracy but in his post 9/11 capacity as commander in chief" (Massumi 2015: 21). Bush authorized the use of the national guard, some of which had recently been fighting in Iraq, to work alongside elements of the US Army that had just returned from fighting in Afghanistan. Having authorized the use of American military force, normally deployed overseas, within the domestic jurisdiction of the United States, Bush then outsourced the assistance-provision role played by the US Government to commercial operators, adding his breath to "the gale winds of enterprising investment following eagerly upon those of Katrina. The aim was less security-assuring than productivity-boosting" (Massumi 2015: 50–51).

Laws are enlisted, too, in this effort to secure humanity in the face of ecological catastrophe. Just as the rule of law has been used to prohibit and criminalize certain uses of armed force, laws have also been designed to prohibit and criminalize acts that harm the environment. "Environmental crime is a broad concept," Neil Boister explains:

> that covers a range of different activities. It involves the trafficking of valuable natural resources through, for example, illegal fishing, the illegal trade in wildlife, and illegal logging and timber smuggling. Environmental crime also involves polluting activities, such as smuggling of ozone-depleting substances and the illegal movement and dumping of toxic waste. Usually large in scale and transnational in nature, environmental crime is facilitated by weak regulation and corruption, and impacts negatively on both the environment and economy in developed and developing states. International regulation of these actions has developed in two stages. Initially

> states adopted measures to prevent the legal pursuit of these activities. They have followed this up with what is now a recognized strategy in international environmental law, the application of penal measures to non-state actors. (2012: 118–119)

Others call for stronger measures, however. Warning that "the new dangers of the Anthropocene have the potential to cause massive global and intergenerational damage to human security" (McKinnon 2017: 411) Catriona McKinnon argues for the extension of the rule of international criminal law to include a new crime that she calls *postericide*; that is, "intentional or reckless conduct fit to bring about the near extinction of humanity" (405). Tim Lindgren goes further still by calling attention to the crime of ecocide—which is defined as "the extensive damage to, destruction of or loss of ecosystem(s) of a given territory, whether by human agency or by other causes, to such an extent that peaceful enjoyment by the inhabitants of that territory has been severely diminished" (2018: 526)—alongside the efforts of those who wish to include this crime in the Rome Statute for the International Criminal Court. Lindgren laments the shortcomings of the rule of law project, which he notes developed in large part alongside the rise of modern industrialized society, when it comes to offering protection to human and non-human life:

> Earth is not protected based on an independent right to life, nor are distinct groups of people. That is, distinct ecological and social *life-systems* that uphold unique ways of life, modes of organization, and modes of existence have no or limited right to existence within international law. These are 'systems of living'—such as ecosystems and indigenous groups—whose existential cognizance differ from that of modern industrial societies, and whose very physical and cultural elements that define them as such. Due to widespread ecological destruction across the planet, these unique and 'alternative' life-systems are facing systematic destruction as ecological harm erodes the necessary conditions that maintain their existence. (2018: 527)

Criminalizing ecocide, and focusing on the nexus between harming the environment and deliberately inflicting on group conditions of life calculated to bring about its physical destruction in whole or in part (an ingredient in the crime of genocide), privilege the protection of humanity ahead of protecting the environment for its own sake, though, as Lindgren enthuses, it is a positive first step "in a long journey towards a socioecologically sound planet, requiring a decolonization of the social, political, and economic cognizance of modern industrial societies that drive the destruction of alternative social and ecological life-systems" (2018: 544).

As some policymakers securitize non-human life, including by making headline-grabbing declarations of climate emergencies, this securitization process opens up further opportunities for humans to exert control over the natural world. More than a process whereby the securitizing of nature is one more way of buttressing the position of those already at the helm of contemporary world affairs, these speech acts and discursive practices shape the relationship between humanity and nature. Constructing non-human species as an existential threat to humanity both prolongs and intensifies the modernist tendency to exercise control over the natural world and intensifies humanity's estrangement from nature. It draws much-needed attention away from the inhumane practices that underscore humanity's engagement with non-human species; humanity's self-interested and self-serving inhumanity, unleashed as pain, suffering and cruelty, remain concealed when these practices should be seen, challenging and potentially shifting, our understanding of what it means to be human within the modernist project. Humanity is not, in and of itself, a timeless concept or a fixed category. It is, instead, a political status. Who is, and who is not, considered human is a hugely contentious question, determined in large part by the configurations of power prevailing at certain places at certain times. As the targets of the War on Terror reveal, the political category of human is somewhat porous and its parameters shift, even in the eyes of the law (Youatt 2014). Even as humans change their relationships to other living species, the concept of humanity evolves and "that a growing debt of cruelty is the externality to the evolution of this life form without a name, unless that name is *Homo destructus*" (Boyd 2015: 109).

If left unchecked, these efforts to govern world affairs in the name of humanity and the rights of human beings will continue to degrade our natural habitat, exterminate other species, ruin ecosystems and alter the functioning parameters of the world's life systems. Finding a solution to the world's environmental problems will invariably involve rethinking how humans relate to animals on an ongoing basis and how the power enjoyed by humanity over non-human life can be better exercised in the present moment (Human Animal Research Network Editorial Collective 2015: viii). As the Human Animal Research Editorial Collective put it, "[t]he sense of urgency about human and non-human interactions in the Anthropocene calls for a reassessment of all our relationships with domestic and 'wild' animals, those species that have co-constitutively evolved alongside humans in specific political communities and designated spaces such as the 'wilderness …'" (2015: xii–xiii). A consensus now exists among biologists that most mammals experience "fear, anxiety, surprise, suffering, anger, affection, pleasure, and the feelings associated with sexual attraction and pain" (Bradshaw 2017: 168). They deserve, at minimum, the right to life. There are, however, obvious shortcomings in the current configurations of the relationship between humans and non-humans. The efforts of animal welfare advocates based in various zones of prosperity are, for instance, undermined by the large-scale, systemic production, killing and consumption of non-human animal life that takes place globally. Moreover, animal welfare advocates often represent animals as subjects for humans to manage better, rather than as political actors in their own capacity. This framing of animals as a managerial problem also lies at the heart of conservation parks, public lands and urban centers where wild animals may appear (Youatt 2014: 212).

Of course, a genuine concern for the welfare of animals and the practice of vegetarianism on ethical grounds does not necessarily make for better people—as demonstrated by Adolf Hitler and some of his fellow Nazis who took a very selective approach to ensuring their fellow human beings' well-being (Bradshaw 2017). For Elizabeth Fisher, the "domestication of women followed the initiation of animal keeping, and it was then that men began to control women's reproductive capacity, enforcing chastity and sexual repression. The violation of animals expedited the violation of human beings" (Fisher, cited in Kriyger 2015: 142).

Henry Fairfield Osborn, a scientist, has understood the Anthropocene to be a war more destructive than the Cold War, with its nuclear arsenal positioned to destroy humanity in an act tantamount to species suicide. Osborn warned that:

> the silent war, eventually the most deadly war, was one in which man has indulged for a long time, blindly and unknowingly. The other world-wide war, still continuing, is bringing more widespread distress to the human race than any that has resulted from armed conflict. It contains potentialities of ultimate disaster greater than would follow the misuse of atomic power. The other war is man's conflict with nature. (Osborn cited in Bonneuil and Fressoz 2016: 282)

On 1 December 2019, the eve of the COP25 climate change talks in Madrid, the Secretary-General of the United Nations, Antonio Guterres, declared "that humanity's war on nature must end" and stated that "We are confronted now with a global climate crisis and the point of no return is no longer over the horizon—it is in sight and hurtling towards us" (2019).

Alternative Futures?

So, then, how might this politico-cultural war on nature be ended? Five factors merit consideration by the world's policymakers. Firstly, political leaders could consider refraining from their rhetorical efforts to securitize nature and other life forms as well as begin de-securitizing climate change and other natural phenomenon by re-politicizing such issues. Secondly, political leaders and their communities could consider valorizing the life of non-human species, especially where those species feel emotions and exercise intellect by taking more seriously their right to life and liberty (and other rights) and more strongly respecting those rights in practice. Thirdly, political leaders could consider granting animals a collective sovereignty based on the right to non-interference, though the recognition and guaranteeing of such rights and associated territory underscores the asymmetrical power relationship between human and non-human (Youatt 2014: 220). Fourthly, political leaders and their communities could start to think of human beings as a species of political animal, which may, in turn, limit our propensity for cruel acts to other non-human species and for humans who have been denied their humanity in various circumstances (214). Lastly, political leaders and their communities could consider compensating for humanity's estrangement from nature by becoming feral in the sense meant by George Mobiot when he argued in favor of rewilding humanity in the following terms:

> Rewilding, to me, is about resisting the urge to control nature and allowing it to find its own way … some people see rewilding as a human retreat from nature; I see it as a re-involvement. I would like to see the reintroduction into the wild not only wolves, Lynx, wolverines, beavers, boar, moose, bison and—perhaps one day in the distant future—elephants and other species, but also human beings. In other words, I see rewilding as an

> enhanced opportunity for people to engage with and delight in the natural world. (2014: 9–11)

That is not to say, however, that the answers to modernity's existential crises are to be found somewhere in the untouched wilderness. While the notion of a pristine wilderness existing beyond modern urban life has provided strong motivation for many environmentalists, it functions symbolically as a refuge from human destruction, pollution and disease, and an antidote to the pathologies of western, industrialized modernity. Despite the alluring quality of such a vision, the realities of the wilderness are less sanguine and, for some, manifest false hope that humanity can reconcile with nature without having to undergo any introspection or a fundamental reinvention of what it means to be human where the human species is one species among many. For others, the pristine wilderness is a mere fantasy that absolves humanity from its culpability for the current state of world affairs, as though it is possible to put aside a five-hundred-year long history of cruel wrongdoing that includes exploitation and neglect and start afresh. Such fantasies are dreamt of by people who, living much if not all of their lives within urban centers, have never actually toiled in soil. The shortcomings inherent in such a vision of the wilderness, held in the imaginations of those whose relationship to nature has already been torn asunder, are evident in the absence of human beings sustaining themselves off the land. Such visions also underscore the distinctiveness of humanity compared to other species, rather than building on common ground, precluding an understanding of what a humanity re-embedded into nature might look like. Ultimately, notions of a pristine environment existing beyond modernity's shadow are disingenuous means of justifying our currents ways of living. Similarly, efforts to protect certain endangered species, which function as a synecdoche for species diversity more generally, serve as false surrogates for nature itself. Moreover, nature's splendor is not confined to remote areas of untouched and uninhabited wilderness; the plants in our gardens or in nearby parks are worthy of our respect too (Cronon 1995).

While there are strong reasons why modernity's silent war on nature should end, I remain somewhat pessimistic because it requires a paradigm shift of near-global reach and an array of vested interested and other factors restraining such efforts appear to be more powerful, at least for the time being. The world's existing governance architecture is too deeply invested in the modernist project, its way of seeing the world, its current paradigm, to change, though as Tarnas points out:

> … the very possibility of a new world view's appearance rests on the underlying archetypal dynamic of the larger culture. Thus, the Copernican revolution that emerged during the Renaissance and Reformation perfectly reflected the archetypal moment of modern humanity's birth out of the ancient-medieval cosmic-ecclesiastical womb. And at the other end, the twentieth century's massive and radical breakdown of so many structures—cultural, philosophical, scientific, religious, moral, artistic, social, economic, political, atomic, ecological—all this suggest the necessary destruction prior to a new birth … . The collective psyche seems to be in the grip of a powerful archetypal dynamic in which the long-awaited modern mind is breaking though, out of the contractions of its birth process, out of which Blake called its 'mind-forg'd manacles,' to rediscover its intimate relationship with nature and the larger cosmos. (1991: 439–440)

The violence, suffering and discord that characterizes modernity's relationship with nature, and the silence engulfing this complex issue, signals the urgent need to reframe how we understand not only the concepts of, and practices surrounding, human rights, law and war but also the often neglected, yet nonetheless important, non-human stakes involved in protecting those rights in times of strife during the conduct of contemporary world affairs. We need, in other words, to loosen the grip of the "mind-forg'd manacles" of those policymakers, their officials and members of civil society whose real-world activities can, at least, ameliorate modernity's sharpest edges.

Moreover, as David Chandler has argued, a sustained critique of humanity's hubristic belief in its own freedom would merely see humans genuflect "before the alter of life as complexity" (2014: 184). While those entrenched in western modernity believe human ingenuity and agency can master and transform the natural world, those who embrace notions of post-human complexity and resilience declare the "war on nature" to be over, believing humanity will become increasingly aware of its embedded attachment to the nature as people govern themselves in self-reflexive ways. For Chandler, however, humanity will likely become even less attached to nature, which will inevitably become strange and mysterious as we are alienated from it. Nature is, it seems, no longer understood as an external setting to be conquered, or even a habitat for humanity. Humanity itself transforms from a species of political animal, distinguished for its internal social struggles for control over the knowable, and sometimes unknowable, materiality of the world, to subjects that no longer act upon the world. The more the humanity and nature become estranged, the more that humans become unrecognizable. More recently, Chander has argued that "[t]he Anthropocene is not mere the recognition of the importance of climate change or global warming; but neither is it merely a critique of modernity; it is affirmed as a new framework for understanding and acting in a world, which can never be considered a 'home'" (2018: 193).

Conclusion

Despite strong reasons explaining why modernity's silent war on nature should end and give way to a peaceful coexistence between humanity and non-human life forms, a peace based on a stronger respect for the rights of other life forms, an array of vested interested and other factors, including entrenched social attitudes about humanity's superiority over all other species and its mastery over nature, restraining such efforts appear to be more powerful, at least for the time being. Humans look set to remain the dominant predator on earth (Bradshaw 2017), residing at the apex of a food chain that systemically exploits the populations of non-human species in inhumane and extremely cruel ways, even as the politico-cultural project of modernity, distinguished by humanity's widespread use of its faculty of reason as cultural practice, destroys the world it shares with other life forms. Having pleaded for the right to life of non-human life forms to be taken seriously and more strongly respected in practice, perhaps through efforts to re-wild humanity, I now close out this book by calling for the academic discipline of International Relations to decenter human affairs in its analyses and transform its research-led inquiries into a misanthropic study of the conduct of contemporary world affairs.

Notes

1. The UDHR's thirty rights are: (1) Right to Equality; (2) Freedom from Discrimination; (3) Right to Life, Liberty, and Personal Security; (4) Freedom from Slavery; (5) Freedom from Torture and Degrading Treatment; (6) Right to Recognition as a Person before the Law; (7) Right to Equality before the Law; (8) Right to Remedy by Competent Tribunal; (9) Freedom from Arbitrary Arrest and Exile; (10) Right to a

Fair Public Hearing; (11) Right to be Considered Innocent until Proven Guilty; (12) Freedom from Interference with Privacy, Family, Home, and Correspondence; (13) Right to Free Movement in and out of the Country; (14) Right to Asylum in other Countries from Persecution; (15) Right to a Nationality and the Freedom to Change It; (16) Right to Marriage and Family; (17) Right to Own Property; (18) Freedom of Belief and Religion; (19) Freedom of Opinion and Information; (20) Right of Peaceful Assembly and Association; (21) Right to Participate in Government and in Free Elections; (22) Right to Social Security; (23) Right to Desirable Work and to Join Trade Unions; (24) Right to Rest and Leisure; (25) Right to Adequate Living Standard; (26) Right to Education; (27) Right to Participate in the Cultural Life of Community; (28) Right to a Social Order that Articulates this Document; (29) Community Duties Essential to Free and Full Development and (30) Freedom from State or Personal Interference in the above Rights. (Kaplan 2018, Table 8.1: 206).

2. International Covenant on Economic, Social and Cultural Rights, GA Res 2200 A (16 December 1966); and the International Covenant on Civil and Political Rights, GA Res 2200 A (16 December 1966).
3. These core human rights treaties are: International Convention on the Elimination of all Forms of Racial Discrimination, 66 UNTS 195 (21 December 1965); Convention on the Elimination of All Forms of Discrimination against Women, GA Res 34/180 (18 December 1979); Convention against Torture and Other Cruel, Inhuman or Degrading Treatment or Punishment, GA Res 39/46 (10 December 1984); the Convention of the Rights of the Child, GA Res 44/25 (20 November 1989); International Convention on the Protection of All Migrant Workers and Members of Their Families, GA Res 45/158 (18 December 1990); the Convention on the Rights of Persons with Disabilities, GA Res 61/106 (13 December 2006); and the International Convention for the Protection of All Persons from Enforced Disappearance, GA Res 61/177 (20 December 2006) (Rodley 2010, 790: fn 31).
4. The European Convention on Human Rights; The American Convention on Human Rights; African Charter on Human and Peoples' Rights, Inter-American Convention to prevent and punish torture, African Charter on the Rights and Welfare of the Child, 1987 European Convention for the Prevention of Torture and Inhuman or Degrading Treatment or Punishment, CETS No. 126.
5. These are: Committee on the Elimination of Racial Discrimination; Committee on Economic, Social and Cultural Rights, Human Rights Committee; Committee on the Elimination of Discrimination against Women; the Committee against Torture; Committee on the Protection of All Migrant Workers and Members of their Families; the Committee on

the Rights of Persons with Disabilities; and the Committee on Enforced Disappearances (Rodley 2010: 808).
6. Incidentally, the efficiencies delivered through using these assembly-line techniques to pack meat were enough to inspire other industrial ventures, including Henry Ford's mass production of motor vehicles.
7. The process of securitization entails all of those individuals and groups who, wielding power over their own communities, can elevate particular issues, which are normally dealt with by the more-or-less routine structures and processes governing the political life of those communities, to the domain of a security issue by representing that particular phenomenon as an existential threat to the political community. Through a speech act, or recurring rhetorical practices, that use a hieratical register, powerful individuals and groups can transform a previously-considered demotic issue into something requiring an exceptional response. The intention of the speech-act author must, however, be received and accepted, at least in part, by his or her wider audience (see Waever 1995; Balzacq 2010; Neal 2019).

References

Balzacq T (2010) Constructivism and Securitization Studies. In The Routledge Handbook of Security Studies, eds. Cavelty MD and Mauer V, 56–72. Routledge, London and New York.

Bigo D and Tsoukala A, eds. (2008) Terror, Insecurity and Liberty: Illiberal Practices of Liberal Regimes After 9/11. Routledge, New York and London.

Boister N (2012) An Introduction to Transnational Criminal Law. Oxford University Press, Oxford.

Bonneuil C and Fressoz JB (2016) The Shock of the Anthropocene. Verso, London and New York.

Boyd M (2015) A Game of Horseshoes for the Anthropocene: The Matter of Externalities of Cruelty to the Horseracing Industry. In Animals in the Anthropocene: Critical Perspectives on Non-Human Futures, eds. The Human Animal Research Network Editorial Collective, 107–134. Sydney University Press, Sydney.

Bradshaw J (2017) The Animals Among US: The New Science of Anthrozoology. Allen Lane, London.

Chandler D (2014) Resilience: The Governance of Complexity. Routledge, London and New York.

Chandler D (2018) Ontopolitics in the Anthropocene: An Introduction to Mapping, Sensing and Hacking. Routledge, New York and London.

Climate Emergency Declarations, www.cedamia.org/global, last accessed 4 September 2020.

Cortright D (2008) Peace: A History of Movements and Ideas. Cambridge University Press, Cambridge.
Cronon W (1995) The Trouble with Wilderness or, Getting Back to the Wrong Nature. In Uncommon Ground: Towards Reinventing Nature, ed. Cronon W, 7–28. W.W. Norton, New York.
Grove JV (2019) Savage Ecology: War and Geopolitics at the End of the World. Duke University Press, Durham and London.
Guterres A (2019) Remarks at the Opening Ceremony of the UN Climate Change Conference (COP25), www.un.org/sg/en/content/sh/speeches/2019-12-02/remarks-opening-ceremony-of-cop23, accessed 3 September 2020.
Harrington C (2016) The Ends of the World: International Relations and the Anthropocene, Millennium—Journal of International Studies 44(3): 478-498.
Human Animal Research Network Editorial Collective (2015) Animals in the Anthropocene: Critical Perspectives on Non-Human Futures. University of Sydney, Sidney.
Kaplan SD (2018) Human Rights in Thick and Thin Society: Universality Without Uniformity. Cambridge University Press, Cambridge.
Kirjner D (2015) Painfully, from the First-Person Singular to First-Person Plural: The Role of Feminism in the Study of the Anthropocene. In Animals in the Anthropocene: Critical Perspectives on Non-Human Futures, eds. Human Animal Research Network Editorial Collective, 153–150. University of Sydney, Sidney.
Latour B (2004) Politics of Nature: How to Bring the Sciences into Democracy, trans. C Porter. Harvard University Press, Cambridge, Massachusetts.
Latour B (2017) Down to Earth: Politics in the New Climatic Regime. Polity, Cambridge.
Lindgren T (2018) Ecocide, Genocide and the Disregard of Alternative Life-Systems. The International Journal of Human Rights 22(4): 525–549.
Massumi B (2015) Ontopower: War, Powers, and the State of Exception. Duke University Press, Durham and London.
McKinnon C (2017) Endangering Humanity: An International Crime? Canadian Journal of Philosophy 27(2–3): 395–415.
Neal AW (2019) Security as Politics: Beyond the State of Exception. Edinburgh University Press, Edinburgh.
O'Manique C and Fourie P (2010) Security and Health in the Twenty-First Century. In The Routledge Handbook of Security Studies, eds. Cavelty MD and Mauer V, 243–253. Routledge, New York and London.
Pettman R (2010) World Affairs: An Analytical Overview. World Scientific, Singapore.

Reus-Smit R (2013) Individual Rights and the Making of the International System. Cambridge University Press, Cambridge.
Rodley N (2010) International Human Rights Law. In International Law (4th ed), ed. Evans MD, 783–818. Oxford University Press, Oxford.
Tarnas R (1991) The Passion of the Western Mind: Understanding the Ideas That Have Shaped Our World View. Pimlico, London.
Waever O (1995) "Securitization and Desecuritization." In On Security, ed. Lipschutz R, 46–86. Columbia University Press, New York.
Williams P (2010) Organized Crime, Drug Trafficking and Trafficking in Women. In The Routledge Handbook of Security Studies, eds. Cavelty MD and Mauer V, 149–158. Routledge, New York and London.
Youatt R (2014) Interspecies Relations, International Relations: Rethinking Anthropocentric Politics. Millennium—Journal of International Studies 43(1): 207–223.

CHAPTER 5

Conclusion

Abstract This concluding chapter not only summarises the preceding argument but also situates the political analysis at the heart of that argument within the academic discipline of International Relations. The chapter calls for disciplinary IR to broaden its focus beyond its current preoccupation with states, economies, and societies in such a way that transforms itself into the misanthropic study of contemporary world affairs. This transformation would require many practitioners of the discipline to recognise their own callous disregard for the politics of non-human species, which reflects and enacts an entrenched anthropocentricism. It remains to be seen if the widespread extinction of life systems and life forms is a catastrophe sufficiently grave to prompt a radical rethinking of the practices that constitute humanity.

Keyword Disciplinary IR · Misanthropy · World affairs · Extinction · Non-human species

The central argument of this book is that the politics of war, international law and human rights produce serious global insecurities. The problem of war, I argued, lies with those individuals and groups who, currently at the helm of world affairs, keep questions of war separate from the

D. Rogers, *Wars, Laws, Rights and the Making of Global Insecurities*, Human Rights Interventions,
https://doi.org/10.1007/978-3-030-90162-2_5

routine politics of international life. The trouble with international law is, I argued, that the most serious of struggles occurring within these social fields are determined by configurations of power that are largely exterior to those fields. In fact, these fields of law are buttressed by the armed force used to sustain a control paradigm that guarantees the security of those who reside comfortably within the world's zones of prosperity. Action taken to promote and protect human rights at a time of ecological catastrophe—action, that is, which place humans as primus inter pares among all life forms on this planet—stimulates modernity's pathological tendencies. I lamented that, while there are strong reasons why modernity's war on nature must end, an array of factors precluding that initiative appear to be more powerful. This state of affairs is not due to some grand conspiracy among a global elite to defraud humanity, as it is a lack of genuine leadership and coherence in the governance of world affairs. In this final chapter, I call for the academic discipline of International Relations (IR) to broaden and deepen its focus beyond its current preoccupation with the state, the economy and society, and to transform itself into misanthropic study of the conduct of contemporary world affairs.

While some scholars suggest disciplinary IR is distinguished by its research agenda that meditates upon the term "international" (Aradau et al. 2015; Ferguson and Mansbach 2007; Darby 2004), others describe it as an American social science (Hoffman 1987; Krippendorf 1987; Smith 2000, 2002). As an American social science, disciplinary IR would not be possible without the financial support of the United States Department of Defense, which has provided incentives for policy-relevant research and has shaped the range of themes investigated and methodologies used in IR scholarship (Grove 2019). A deeper understanding of disciplinary IR is that it constitutes a field of teaching and research that comprises contending explanations of the politics of contemporary world affairs. Understood in this way, IR is well placed to enable those researchers who wish to better understand and more cogently explain the politics behind, and the complex relationships among, wars, laws and rights.

Disciplinary IR offers accounts of three main dimensions of contemporary world affairs (Pettman 2001). The politico-strategic dimension of world affairs was the first to be thoroughly explored within the discipline while a second dimension, concerning the affairs of international political economy, began to receive systemic and sustained treatment from about the 1970s onwards. A third dimension coheres around the self-making practices which occur as international political sociology. The mainstream practices that dominate IR create and sustain margins, though those who are marginalized often have important accounts to offer. These marginalized perspectives draw much-needed attention to the centrality of race, ethnicity and indigeneity (Barkawi 2011, 2016; Barkawi and Stanski 2012); class, capital and intensifying inequalities (Berdal and Zaum 2013; Duffield 2014, 2019; Leech 2012; Rogers 2016) and gender and sex (Wilcox 2015; Cohn 2013; Sjoberg 2014, 2016) in the politics of not only of wars but also of international law and human rights.

As an academic discipline, IR emerges out of the modernist project in the long nineteenth century (1776–1914) and is imbued with positivism (Buzan and Lawson 2015). Its rise within modernist universities is facilitated by the rationalist mind gaze, which has, as explained in the previous chapter, contributed to the radical transformation of Earth's ecology. Despite the warnings given by those alarmed by the Anthropocene's harmful impacts on nature—that is, the accelerating rate at which the world's species are becoming extinct, its resources exhausted, its climate warmed, its oceans polluted and its landmass deforested—the fate of the planet remains, strangely, a peripheral political concern for much of humanity, though it is gaining in salience, particularly within intergovernmental organizations with global reach (see, for instance, the United Nations' Intergovernmental Panel on Climate Change's most recent report, Climate Change 2021: The Physical Science Basis 2021). None of the major efforts coordinated among the international community, understood in its widest sense, appears to be bearing much fruit. Indeed, to suggest that the same individuals and groups who have dominated world affairs in a way that made ecocide possible can now solve this deeper and more complex problem "displays a persistent and willful naïveté of how the global was made in the first place" (Grove 2019: 3). Grove goes onto to explain that:

> Global politics for the past five hundred years is proof of the opposite of common sense. There is a centuries-long investment in research, development, and deployment of techniques to ensure that survival is only ever a right for some. This right for some, more often than not, is ensured at the expense of the self-determination and continuation of living for the overwhelming majority of the planet's human population. [...] In fact, it is this very geopolitics—nation-states making decisions and wielding power at a global scale—that the [climate] scientists want to steer away from

> war toward saving the planet, which is not premised at some foundational level on a general principle of order or the good. Geopolitics is, at its most fundamental level, a husbandry of global life in which thriving is intimately connected to the particular form of life and the particular lifeworld through which one becomes who one is. Geopolitics is structured to be selective, and to ensure that selectivity by lethal force. (pp. 2–3)

And that:

> The geopolitical project of planet Earth is a violent pursuit of a form of life at the cost of others—full stop. However, at the same time, with an often zero-sum game over form of life at its center, global war—the presumed opposite of human survival—is not primarily about direct killing. Instead, the violence of geopolitics is an ecological principle of world making that renders some forms of life principle and other forms of life useful or inconsequential. (p. 3)

Understood in this light, it is not surprising that disciplinary International Relations has not engaged fully with the making of these global insecurities, though this field of study concerned with the politics of contemporary world affairs must become more than a study of human affairs if it is to offer meaningful and comprehensive explanations. Since disciplinary IR tends only to concern itself with politics among humans, many IR scholars do not, and will never, care about non-human politics, a disregard fueled in many cases by the enormous disparity in power between even the smallest state and the largest animal community (Youatt 2014).

One reason for this is that the academic discipline of International Relations, like much of the humanities and many of the social sciences, is an extension of an anthropocentricism—namely, a set of ideas that assert "a claim of radical human exceptionality" (Youatt 2014: 209) and state that human beings are more significant than other species and life forms—that drives the politics of war, international law and human rights. This ideology is the result of those rationalist cognitive practices and human relations, already mentioned above, that inflict serious harm on the natural world and drive humanity's estrangement from nature. As anthropocentric thinking meditates upon humanity, it enacts humanity's, limits. While anthropocentrism assumes agreement over what, exactly, constitutes the category of "human" is static, those who are deemed less than "human" either become something closer to beasts in the prisons of

Guantanamo Bay or the camps of Nazi Germany, or remain as untouched natives and uncivilized barbarians conquered as the New World burst into existence. Being "human" has less to do with belonging, biologically, to a species and everything to do with being a member of particular political community (Youatt 2014). This commitment to anthropocentrism also produces and sustains ontological myopia that enacts limits to our collective understanding of the scale and depth of these global insecurities and masks the enormity of the stakes involved.

Such a state of disciplinary affairs needs an urgent remedy, however. Lamenting disciplinary IR's slowness to fully comprehend the challenge posed by the Anthropocene, Harrington (2016) exhorts scholars to rethink their core assumptions of "power" and "the international" and take more seriously the ways in which humanity, was estranged from but remains entangled in the natural world. The explanatory task is an urgent one because the existence of the Anthropocene is a direct result of current modalities of world affairs, including the prevailing states-based system. The Anthropocene's wake contains the conditions of possibility for humanity's, extinction, or near extinction, which ought to prompt a reconsideration of traditional security problems that can appear, in contrast, trivial—excepting, of course, the existential threat posed by the existence of thermonuclear weapons (van Munster and Sylvest 2016). It behooves IR scholars to provide more comprehensive accounts of how and why political leaders have allowed the human species to come this close to calamity and for non-human animals, plants and ecosystems to be seriously harmed. Such accounts will require humans to be conceptualized as bounded creatures caught in nature. To do less by carrying on as business-as-usual under such alarming conditions is, according to Harrington, "a dangerous form of denialism and moral failure" (2016: 481).

However, Grove (2019) alerts researchers to the dangers of thinking through anthropocentrism, rather than thinking on it, by reminding us that the crisis manifested in the Anthropocene obscures the configurations of power and the ancillary practices of violence that have created the present calamity just as a narrow focus on climate change erases the role played by the United States in fostering the current international status quo. Grove suggests that IR scholars eschew a research agenda informed by a presumption of what ought to be studied when this merely extends the trajectory of existing research, and favor instead our own attentiveness to the changing world around us and how it might be studied anew.

We might see that the politics animating contemporary world affairs is a global war that produces:

> … a savage ecology, radically antagonistic to survival as a collective rather than discriminatory goal … . the line between extreme human misery and just transformation is not practically or impractically out of reach because of a lack of will or misuse of resources. For the majority of the planet, the failure to ensure survival is not about an oversight or bad financial management. Instead, the line between misery and something else is heavily policed and enforced with everything, from odious international debt to hell fire missiles. (p. 4)

To break this impasse, those who advance understanding by producing knowledge on the politics of contemporary world affairs need to write into their analysis non-human encounters and experiences. The academic discipline of International Relations needs to decenter human affairs in its analyses and to transform its research-led inquiries into a misanthropic study of the politics of contemporary world affairs, as if non-human species life mattered.[1] I am not alone in calling for this change. Bonneuil and Fressoz plead for a "new environmental humanities to rethink our visions of the world and our ways of inhabiting the Earth together" (2016: xii).

Casting light on humanity's pathological relationship to nature and non-human species is an important step. If the structures and processes of human politics continue to render that pathology opaque, then IR scholars need to abandoned those analytical devices as well their other anthropocentric commitments. Such rethinking might include the embrace of what Grove calls "feral reasoning … a renewed sense of adventure and creativity in pursuit only of itself. Feral is not a way out of all this, but rather a way through" (2019: 11). This will also require turning away from understanding the conduct of contemporary world affairs as politics among humans, toward understanding world affairs as interspecies politics that gives focus to a variety of human-non-human encounters and relations, and to their significance in the context of planetary life. "[B]y breaking down received ideas about the political that have contributed to the current set of ecological, animal and biopolitical crises," Youatt maintains, "thinking in interspecies terms can begin to broach new and important questions about what it means to live well with others, and why power, violence and difference function in the ways that they do" (2014: 222). This would mean that world affairs are properly understood as encompassing all of the world and its multitudinous life forms.

The stakes here are no less than a reduction in the scale and intensity of today's most pressing global insecurities, but this requires a rethinking of what it means to remain human among the ruins of our current habitat. We must consider, as Grove insists we should, discarding the concept of the Anthropocene and inventing ourselves afresh, as a new species with a new set of political practices whose central purpose is to find a novel mode of existence and, hopefully, survival (2019: 11).

Note

1. I deliberately echo E.F. Schumacher's provocative critique of modern economics, *Small Is Beautiful: A Study of Economic as if People Mattered*, which suggested a "Buddhist economics must be very different from the economics of modern materialism, since the Buddhist sees the essence of civilization not in the multiplications of wants, but in the purification of human character" (1973: 40).

References

Aradau C, Huysmans J, Neal A, and Voelkner N, eds. (2015) Critical Security Methods: New Frameworks for Analysis. Routledge, London and New York.

Barkawi T (2011) From War to Security: Security Studies, the Wider Agenda, and the Fate of the Study of War. Millennium: Journal of International Studies 39(3): 701.

Barkawi T (2016) Decolonising War. European Journal of International Security 1(2): 199.

Barkawi T and Stanski K, eds (2012) Orientalism and War. Hurst & Company, London.

Berdal M and Zaum D, eds. (2013) Political Economy of State-Building: Power After Peace. Routledge, New York and London.

Bonneuil C and Fressoz JB (2016) The Shock of the Anthropocene. Verso, London and New York.

Buzan B and Lawson G (2015) The Global Transformation: History, Modernity and the Making of International Relations. Cambridge University Press, Cambridge.

Cohn C, ed. (2013) Women and War. Polity, Cambridge.

Darby P (2004) Pursing the Political: A Postcolonial Rethinking of Relations 'International'. Millennium: Journal of International Studies 33(1): 1.
Duffield M (2014) Global Governance and the New Wars: The Merging of Development and Security. Zed, London.
Duffield M (2019) Post-Humanitarianism: Governing Precarity in the Digital World. Polity, Cambridge.
Ferguson Y and Mansbach RW (2007) Post-Internationalism and IR Theory. Millennium: Journal of International Studies 35: 529.
Grove JV (2019) Savage Ecology: War and Geopolitics at the End of the World. Duke University Press, Durham and London.
Harrington C (2016) The Ends of the World: International Relations and the Anthropocene. Millennium—Journal of International Studies 44(3): 478–498.
Hoffman S (1987) An American Social Science: International Relations. Reprinted in eds. Janus and Minerva: Essays in the Theory and Practice of International Politics. Worldview Press, Boulder.
Krippendorf E (1987) The Dominance of American Approaches in International Relations. Millennium: Journal of International Studies 16: 202.
Leech G (2012) Capitalism: A Structural Genocide. Zed Books, London.
Pettman R (2001) World Politics: Rationalism and Beyond. Palgrave, New York.
Rogers P (2016) Irregular War: ISIS and the New Threat from the Margins. I.B. Tauris, London and New York.
Schumacher EF (1973) Small Is Beautiful: A Study of Economics as if People Mattered. Vintage, London.
Sjoberg L (2014) Gender, War and Conflict. Polity, Cambridge.
Sjoberg L (2016) Women as Wartime Rapists: Beyond Sensation and Stereotyping. New York University Press, New York.
Smith S (2000) The Discipline of International Relations: Still an American Social Science? Paper presented at the annual conference of the Australian Political Science Association, Canberra, 5 October.
Smith S (2002) The United States and the Discipline of International Relations: "Hegemonic Country, Hegemonic Discipline". International Studies Review 4(2): 67.
van Munster R and Sylvest C (2016) Nuclear Realism: Global Political Thought During the Thermonuclear Revolution. Routledge, New York and London.
Wilcox LB (2015) Bodies of Violence: Theorizing Embodied Subjects in International Relations. Oxford University Press, Oxford.
Youatt R (2014) Interspecies Relations, International Relations: Rethinking Anthropocentric Politics. Millennium—Journal of International Studies 43(1): 207–223.

Bibliography

Adler-Nissen R, ed. (2013) Bourdieu in International Relations: Rethinking Key Concepts in IR. Routledge, London and New York.

Adshead SAM (2004) T'ang China: The Rise of the East in World History. Palgrave Macmillan, New York.

Alley R (2004) Internal Conflict and the International Community: Wars Without End? Ashgate, Aldershot.

Anghie A (2004) Imperialism, Sovereignty and the Making of International Law. Cambridge University Press, Cambridge.

Amnesty International (2006) Dead on Time—Arms Transportation, Brokering and the Threat to Human Rights. International Secretariat, London.

Aradau C, Huysmans J, Neal A, and Voelkner N, eds. (2015) Critical Security Methods: New Frameworks for Analysis. Routledge, London and New York.

Arendt H (1970) On Violence. Harcourt, Brace and World.

Balzacq T (2010) Constructivism and Securitization Studies. In The Routledge Handbook of Security Studies, eds. Cavelty MD and Mauer V, 56–72. Routledge, London and New York.

Barbay V (2015) The Mater of Death: Posthumous Wildlife Art in the Anthropocene. In Animals in the Anthropocene: Critical Perspectives on Non-Human Futures, eds. Human Animal Research Network Editorial Collective, 89–106. University of Sydney, Sydney.

Barkawi T (2011) From War to Security: Security Studies, the Wider Agenda, and the Fate of the Study of War. Millennium: Journal of International Studies 39(3): 701.

D. Rogers, *Wars, Laws, Rights and the Making of Global Insecurities*, Human Rights Interventions,
https://doi.org/10.1007/978-3-030-90162-2

Barkawi T (2016) Decolonising War. European Journal of International Security 1(2): 199.

Barkawi T and Brighton S (2011) Conclusion: Absent War Studies? War, Knowledge, and Critique. In The Changing Character of War, eds. Strachan H and Scheipers S. Oxford University Press, Oxford.

Barkawi T and Stanski K, eds. (2012) Orientalism and War. Hurst & Company, London.

Berdal M and Zaum D, eds. (2013) Political Economy of State-Building: Power After Peace. Routledge, New York and London.

Bigo D (2011) Pierre Bourdieu and International Relations: Power of Practices, Practices of Power. International Political Sociology 5: 225–258.

Bigo D (2013) Security: Analysing Transnational Professionals of (In)security in Europe. In Bourdieu in International Relations: Rethinking Key Concepts in IR, ed. Adler-Nissen, 114–130. Routledge, New York and London.

Bigo D and Tsoukala A, eds. (2007) Terror, Insecurity and Liberty: Illiberal Practices of Liberal Regimes After 9/11. Routledge, New York and London.

Black J (2015) War in the Modern War, 1990-2014. Routledge, London and New York.

Boister N (2012) An Introduction to Transnational Criminal Law. Oxford University Press, Oxford.

Boister N and Cryer R (2008) Documents on the Tokyo International Military Tribunal: Charter, Indictment and Judgments. Oxford University Press, Oxford.

Bonditti P, Bigo D, and Gros F, eds. (2017) Foucault and the Modern International: Silences and Legacies for the Study of World Politics. Palgrave Macmillan, New York.

Bonneuil C and Fressoz JB (2016) The Shock of the Anthropocene. Verso, London and New York.

Bourdieu P (1987) The Force of Law: Toward a Sociology of the Juridical Field. The Hastings Law Journal 38(July): 814–853.

Boyd M (2015) A Game of Horseshoes for the Anthropocene: The Matter of Externalities of Cruelty to the Horseracing Industry. In Animals in the Anthropocene: Critical Perspectives on Non-Human Futures, eds. The Human Animal Research Network Editorial Collective, 107–134. Sydney University Press, Sydney.

Bradshaw J (2017) The Animals Among US: The New Science of Anthrozoology. Allen Lane, London.

Bull H and Watson A (1984) The Expansion of International Society. Oxford University Press, Oxford.

Buzan B and Lawson G (2015) The Global Transformation: History, Modernity and the Making of International Relations. Cambridge University Press, Cambridge.

Cassese A (2008) International Criminal Law (2nd ed). Oxford University Press, Oxford.
Chandler D (2014) Resilience: The Governance of Complexity. Routledge, London and New York.
Chandler D (2018) Ontopolitics in the Anthropocene: An Introduction to Mapping, Sensing and Hacking. Routledge, New York and London.
Charron A (2011) UN Sanctions and Conflict: Responding to Peace and Security Threats. Routledge, New York.
Chinkin C and Kaldor M (2017) International Law and New Wars. Cambridge University Press, Cambridge.
Clausewitz C (1982; first published 1832) On War. Penguin, London.
Climate Emergency Declarations, www.cedamia.org/global, last accessed 4 September 2020.
Cohn C, ed. (2013) Women and War. Polity, Cambridge.
Cooper J (2008) Raphael Lemkin and the Struggle for the Genocide Convention. Palgrave Macmillan, New York.
Cortright D (2008) Peace: A History of Movements and Ideas. Cambridge University Press, Cambridge.
Cox RW (1984) Social Forces, States and World Orders: Beyond International Relations Theory. In Culture, Ideology, and World Order, ed. Walker RBJ. Westworld Press, Boulder and London.
Crawford E (2015) Identifying the Enemy: Civilian Participation in Armed Conflict. Oxford University Press, Oxford.
Cronon W (1995) The Trouble with Wilderness or, Getting Back to the Wrong Nature. In Uncommon Ground: Towards Reinventing Nature, ed. Cronon W, 7–28. W.W. Norton, New York.
Cryer R, Friman H, Robinson D, and Wilmshurst E, eds. (2010) An Introduction to International Criminal Law and Procedure (2nd ed). Cambridge University Press, Cambridge.
Dallaire R (2010) The Fight Like Soldiers, They Die Like Children. Hutchinson, London.
Danner AM (2001) Constructing a Hierarchy of Crimes in International Law Sentencing. Virginia Law Review 87(3): 415.
Darby P (2004) Pursing the Political: A Postcolonial Rethinking of Relations 'International'. Millennium: Journal of International Studies 33(1): 1.
Dillon, M and Neal A, eds. (2008) Foucault on Politics, Security and War. Palgrave, New York and London.
Duffield M (2014) Global Governance and the New Wars: The Merging of Development and Security. Zed, London.
Duffield M (2019) Post-Humanitarianism: Governing Precarity in the Digital World. Polity, Cambridge.

Dunant H (1939) A Memory of Solferino. International Committee of the Red Cross, Geneva, Switzerland.

Eisenstadt SN (2000) Multiple Modernities. Daedalus 129(1): 1–29.

Fabre C (2012) Cosmopolitan War. Oxford University Press, Oxford.

Falk R (2003) The Great Terror War. Aris Books, Gloucestershire.

Fazal TM (2007) State Death: The Politics and Geography of Conquest, Occupation and Annexation. Princeton University Press, Princeton and Oxford.

Ferguson Y and Mansbach RW (2007) Post-Internationalism and IR Theory. Millennium: Journal of International Studies 35: 529.

Forsythe DJ (2005) The Humanitarians: The International Committee of the Red Cross. Cambridge University Press, Cambridge.

Foucault M (1978) The History of Sexuality, Volume 1: An Introduction. Vintage Books, New York.

Foucault M (2003) "Society Must Be Defended": Lectures at the College de France, 1975–1976, trans. Macey D. Picador, New York.

Galtung J and Jacobsen CG (2000) Searching for Peace: The Road to TRANSCEND. Pluto Press, London and Sterling, Virginia.

Goldhagen DJ (2009) Worse Than War: Genocide, Eliminationism, and the Ongoing Assault on Humanity. Little Brown, London.

Gray J (2007) Black Mass: Apocalyptic Religion and the Death of Utopia. Penguin, London.

Grey C (2010) The Use of Force and the International Legal Order. In International Law (4th ed), ed. Evans M, 618–648. Oxford University Press, Oxford.

Grove JV (2019) Savage Ecology: War and Geopolitics at the End of the World. Duke University Press, Durham and London.

Guterres A (2019) Remarks at the Opening Ceremony of the UN Climate Change Conference (COP25), www.un.org/sg/en/content/sh/speeches/2019-12-02/remarks-opening-ceremony-of-cop23, accessed 3 September 2020.

Harrington C (2016) The Ends of the World: International Relations and the Anthropocene. Millennium—Journal of International Studies 44(3): 478–498.

Harris D and Sivakumaran S (2015) Cases and Materials on International Law. Thomson Reuters, London.

Hoffman S (1987) An American Social Science: International Relations. Reprinted in eds. Janus and Minerva: Essays in the Theory and Practice of International Politics. Worldview Press, Boulder.

Hoffman B (2006) Inside Terrorism (revised and expanded ed). Colombia University Press, New York.

Human Animal Research Network Editorial Collective (2015) Animals in the Anthropocene: Critical Perspectives on Non-Human Futures. University of Sydney, Sidney.

Ish-Shalom P (2019) Beyond the Veil of Knowledge: Triangulating Security, Democracy, and Academic Scholarship. University of Michigan Press, Ann Arbor.

Jabre V (2007) Michel Foucault's Analytics of War: The Social, the International, and the Racial. International Political Sociology 1(1): 67–81, https://doi.org/10.1111/j.1749-5687.2007.00005.

Jackson P (2009) Pierre Bourdieu. In Critical Theorists and International Relations, eds. Edkins J and Vaughan-Williams N, 102–113. Routledge, London and New York.

Kaldor M (2001) New and Old Wars: Organised Violence in a Global Era. Polity, Cambridge.

Kaplan SD (2018) Human Rights in Thick and Thin Society: Universality Without Uniformity. Cambridge University Press, Cambridge.

Keegan J (1993) A History of Warfare. Random House, London.

Kirjner D (2015) Painfully, from the First-Person Singular to First-Person Plural: The Role of Feminism in the Study of the Anthropocene. In Animals in the Anthropocene: Critical Perspectives on Non-Human Futures, eds. Human Animal Research Network Editorial Collective, 153–150. University of Sydney, Sidney.

Kittrie OF (2016) Lawfare: Law as a Weapon of War. Oxford University Press, Oxford.

Klare MT (2002) Resource Wars: The New Landscape of Global Conflict. Henry Holt and Company, New York.

Koskenniemi M (2011) The Politics of International Law. Hart Publishing, Oxford and Portland, Oregon.

Krippendorf E (1987) The Dominance of American Approaches in International Relations. Millennium: Journal of International Studies 16: 202.

Latour B (2004) Politics of Nature: How to Bring the Sciences into Democracy, trans. C Porter. Harvard University Press, Cambridge, Massachusetts.

Latour B (2017) Down to Earth: Politics in the New Climatic Regime. Polity, Cambridge.

Leech G (2012) Capitalism: A Structural Genocide. Zed Books, London.

Lindgren T (2018) Ecocide, Genocide and the Disregard of Alternative Life-Systems. The International Journal of Human Rights 22(4): 525–549.

Lowe V, Roberts A, Welsh J and Zaum D, eds. (2008) The United Nations Security Council and War: The Evolution of Thought and Practice Since 1945. Oxford University Press, Oxford.

Lumpe L, ed. (2000) Running Guns: The Global Black Market in Small Arms. Zed, London.

Luttwak EN (1999) Give War a Chance. Foreign Affairs 78(4) (July–Aug): 36–44.

Martini A (2021) The UN and Counter-Terrorism: Global Hegemonies, Power and Identities. Routledge, New York and London.

Massumi B (2015) Ontopower: War, Powers, and the State of Exception. Duke University Press, Durham and London.

McKinley M (2007) Economic Globalization as Religious War: Tragic Convergence. Routledge, London and New York.

McKinnon C (2017) Endangering Humanity: An International Crime? Canadian Journal of Philosophy 27(2–3): 395–415.

Meltzer BD (2005) Robert H Jackson: Nuremberg's Architect and Advocate. Albany Law Review 68: 55.

Minear RH (1971) Victors' Justice: The Tokyo War Crimes Trial. Princeton University Press, New Jersey.

Monbiot G (2013) Feral: Rewilding the Land, Sea and Human Life. Penguin, London.

Monin L and Gallimore A (2002) The Devil's Gardens: A History of Landmines. Pimlico, London.

Munkler H (2012) Old and New Wars. In The Routledge Handbook of Security Studies, eds. Cavelty MD and Mauer V, 190–199. Routledge, New York and London.

Neal AW (2019) Security as Politics: Beyond the State of Exception. Edinburgh University Press, Edinburgh.

Neal AW (2009) Michael Foucault. In Critical Theorists and International Relations, eds. Edkins J and Vaughan-Williams N, 161–170. Routledge, London and New York.

O'Manique C and Fourie P (2010) Security and Health in the Twenty-First Century. In The Routledge Handbook of Security Studies, eds. Cavelty MD and Mauer V, 243–253. Routledge, New York and London.

Owens P (2015) Economy of Force: Counterinsurgency and the Historical Rise of the Social. Cambridge University Press, Cambridge.

Peres MFT (2004) Firearm-Related Violence in Brazil: Country Report. Centre for the Study of Violence, University of Sao Paulo.

Petterrson T, Hogbladh S and Oberg M (2019) Organized Violence, 1989-2018 and Peace Agreements. Journal of Peace Research 56(94): 589–603.

Petterrson T, Davies S, Deniz A, Engstrom G, Hawach N, Hogbadh S, and Oberg MSM (2021) Organized Violence, 1989-2020, with a Special Focus on Syria. Journal of Peace Research 58(4): 809–825.

Pettman R (2001) World Politics: Rationalism and Beyond. Palgrave, New York.

Pettman R (2004) Reason, Culture, Religion: The Metaphysics of World Politics. Palgrave, New York.

Pettman R (2010) World Affairs: An Analytical Overview. World Scientific, Singapore.
Reid J (2008) Life Struggles: War, Discipline and Biopolitics in the Thought of Michel Foucault. In Foucault on Politics, Security and War, eds. Dillon M and Neal AW, 65–92. Palgrave Macmillan, New York.
Reus-Smit R (2013) Individual Rights and the Making of the International System. Cambridge University Press, Cambridge.
Robertson G (2008) Crimes Against Humanity: The Struggle for Global Justice. Penguin, London.
Rodley N (2010) International Human Rights Law. In International Law (4th ed), ed. Evans MD, 783–818. Oxford University Press, Oxford.
Rogers D (2009) Postinternationalism and Small Arms Control: Theory, Politics, Security. Surrey, Ashgate.
Rogers D (2010) Review Essay: Transforming R2P from Rhetoric to Reality. Genocide Studies and Prevention: An International Journal 5(1) (Spring): 106–113.
Rogers P (2016) Irregular War: ISIS and the New Threat from the Margins. I.B. Tauris, London and New York.
Rogers D (2018) Law, Politics and the Limits of Prosecuting Mass Atrocity. Palgrave Macmillan, New York.
Rosenau JN (1990) Turbulence in World Politics: A Theory of Change and Continuity. Princeton University Press, New Jersey.
Sandberg B (2016) War and Conflict in the Early Modern World, 1500-1700. Polity, Cambridge.
Sanders R (2018) Plausible Legality: Legal Culture and Political Imperative in the Global War on Terror. Oxford University Press, Oxford.
Schabas W (2012) Unimaginable Atrocities: Justice, Politics, and Rights at the War Crimes Tribunals. Oxford University Press, Oxford.
Schmitt C (1937) The Turn to the Discriminating Concept of War. In Carl Schmitt Writing on War, ed. and trans. Nunan T. Polity, Cambridge.
Schumacher EF (1973) Small Is Beautiful: A Study of Economics as If People Mattered. Vintage, London.
Sellars K (2013) 'Crimes Against Peace' and International Law. Cambridge University Press, Cambridge.
Simpson G (2004) Great Powers and Outlaw States: Unequal Sovereigns in the International Legal Order. Cambridge University Press, Cambridge.
Simpson G (2007) Law, War and Crime: War Crime Trials and the Reinvention of International Law. Polity, Cambridge.
Sjoberg L (2014) Gender, War and Conflict. Polity, Cambridge.
Sjoberg L (2016) Women as Wartime Rapists: Beyond Sensation and Stereotyping. New York University Press, New York.

Slye RC and Van Schaack B (2009) International Criminal Law. Aspen Publishers, New York.

Smith S (2000) The Discipline of International Relations: Still an American Social Science? Paper presented at the annual conference of the Australian Political Science Association, Canberra, 5 October.

Smith S (2002) The United States and the Discipline of International Relations: "Hegemonic Country, Hegemonic Discipline". International Studies Review 4(2): 67.

Struett MJ (2008) The Politics of Constructing the International Criminal Court: NGOs, Discourse, and Agency. Palgrave Macmillan, New York.

Tarnas R (1991) The Passion of the Western Mind: Understanding the Ideas That Have Shaped Our World View. Pimlico, London.

Teitel RG (2011) Humanity's Law. Oxford University Press, Oxford.

Terdiman R (1987) Translator's Introduction for 'The Force of Law: Towards a Sociology of the Juridical Field' by Pierre Bourdieu in The Hastings Law Journal 38(July): 805–813.

Thirlway H (2010) The Sources of International Law. In International Law (4th ed), ed. Evans M. Oxford University Press, Oxford.

Tilly C (1992) Coercion, Capital, and European States, Ad 990-1992. Blackwell, Cambridge and Oxford.

Toulmin S (1990) Cosmopolis: The Hidden Agenda of Modernity. University of Chicago Press, Chicago.

Turns D (2010) The Law of Armed Conflict (International Humanitarian Law). In International Law (4th ed), ed. Evans M. Oxford University Press, Oxford.

van Munster R and Sylvest C (2016) Nuclear Realism: Global Political Thought During the Thermonuclear Revolution. Routledge, New York and London.

Vasquez JA (2009) The War Puzzle Revisited. Cambridge University Press, Cambridge.

Waever O (1995) Securitization and Desecuritization. In On Security, ed. Lipschutz R, 46–86. Columbia University Press, New York.

Weber (2001) The Protestant Ethic and the Spirit of Capitalism [1904]. Routledge, New York.

Wessells M (2006) Child Soldiers: From Violence to Protection. Harvard University Press, Cambridge, Massachusetts.

Wilcox LB (2015) Bodies of Violence: Theorizing Embodied Subjects in International Relations. Oxford University Press, Oxford.

Wilkinson P (2010) Terrorism. In The Routledge Handbook of Security Studies, eds. Cavelty MD and Mauer V. Routledge, London and New York.

Williams P (2010) Organized Crime, Drug Trafficking and Trafficking in Women. In The Routledge Handbook of Security Studies, eds. Cavelty MD and Mauer V, 149–158. Routledge, New York and London.

Willms J (2015) Courts of Armed Groups—A Tool for Inducing Higher Compliance with International Humanitarian Law? In Inducing Compliance with International Humanitarian Law: Lessons from the Great Lakes Region, ed. Kriger H. Cambridge University Press, Cambridge.

Wilson PH (2009) The Thirty Years War: Europe's Tragedy. Belknap Press of Harvard University Press, Cambridge, Massachusetts.

Youatt R (2014) Interspecies Relations, International Relations: Rethinking Anthropocentric Politics. Millennium—Journal of International Studies 43(1): 207–223.

Zehfuss M (2018) War and the Politics of Ethics. Oxford University Press, Oxford.

Zolo, D (2009) Victors' Justice: From Nuremberg to Baghdad. Verso, London and New York.

Official Reports

Keenan JB (1946) Opening Statement of the Prosecution Northcroft Archive (Prosecution's Document file) Macmillan Brown Library, University of Canterbury, New Zealand.

2001 Report of the International Commission on Intervention and State Sovereignty (ICISS).

The National Security Strategy of the United States of America (2002) Washington DC: The White House.

The Report of the UN Secretary-General's High-Level Panel on Threats, Challenges, and Change, *A More Secure World: Our Shared Responsibility* (2004).

UN Secretary-General Kofi Annan, *In Larger Freedom: Toward Development, Security and Human Rights for All* (2005).

United Nations' Intergovernmental Panel on Climate Change (2021) Climate Change 2021: The Physical Science Basis, available at https://www.ipcc.ch/assessment-report/ar6/.

United Nations Office for Disarmament Affairs (2018) *Securing Our Common Future: An Agenda for Disarmament.* New York.

Weapons of Mass Destruction Commission (2006) *Weapons of Terror: Freeing the World of Nuclear, Biological and Chemical Arms.* Stockholm.

Instruments of International Law

Arab Convention on the Suppression of Terrorism (1998).

Biological Weapons Convention (1972).

Charter of the United Nations (1945).

Covenant of the League of Nations (1919).

Convention on the Prevention and Punishment of the Crime of Genocide (1948).
Convention of the Organisation of the Islamic Conference on Combating International Terrorism (1999).
Convention for the Suppression of Unlawful Seizure of Aircraft (1970).
Convention for the Suppression of Unlawful Acts Against the Safety of Civil Aviation (1971) and Its Protocol for the Suppression of Unlawful Acts of Violence at Airports Serving International Civil Aviation (1988).
Convention on the Prevention and Punishment of Crimes Against Internationally Protected Persons, Including Diplomatic Persons (1973).
Convention on the Physical Protection of Nuclear Material (1980).
Convention on the Suppression of Unlawful Acts Against the Safety of Maritime Navigation (1988) and Its Protocol for the Suppression of Unlawful Acts Against the Safety of Fixed Platforms Located on the Continental Shelf (1988).
Convention on Certain Conventional Weapons (1980).
Chemical Weapons Convention (1993).
Convention on the Prohibition of the Use, Stockpiling, Production and Transfer of Anti-Personnel Mines and on their Destruction (1997).
Convention on Cluster Munitions (2008).
Convention Against Torture and Other Cruel, Inhumane or Degrading Treatment or Punishment (1984).
Charter of the International Military for the Far East (as amended 26 April 1946) as reproduced in Boister N and Cryer R (2008) Documents on the Tokyo International Military Tribunal: Charter, Indictment and Judgments. Oxford: Oxford University Press.
European Convention on the Suppression of Terrorism (1977).
European Convention on the Prevention of Terrorism (2005).
General Treaty for the Renunciation of War as an Instrument of National Policy (1928).
Geneva Conventions; Common Article 3 of the Geneva Conventions; Additional Protocol II.
Geneva Protocol (1925).
Geneva Conventions of 1864, of 1949 and the supplementary Protocols of 1977.
International Convention against the Taking of Hostages (1979).
International Convention for the Suppression of Terrorist Bombings (1997).
International Convention for the Suppression of the Financing of Terrorism (1999).
International Convention for the Suppression of Acts of Nuclear Terrorism (2005).

International Military Tribunal (1947) Trial of the Major War Criminals before the International Military Tribunal II Proceedings, 14 November–30 November 1945. Nuremberg, Germany.
London Agreement of 8 August 1945—with the Charter of the International Military Tribunal in International Military Tribunal Trial of the Major War Criminals before the International Military Tribunal, Nuremberg 14 November 1945–1 October 1946 Nuremberg, Germany.
OAS Convention to Prevent and Punish Acts of Terrorism Taking the Form of Crimes against Persons and Related Extortion that are of International Significance (1971).
OAU Convention on the Prevention and Combating of Terrorism (1999).
Rome Statute of the International Criminal Court (1998).
Statute of the International Criminal Tribunal for the Prosecution of Persons Responsible for Serious Violations of International Humanitarian Law Committed in the Territory of the Former Yugoslavia since 1991 (1994).
Statute of the International Criminal Tribunal for the Prosecution of Persons Responsible for Genocide and Other Serious Violations of International Humanitarian Law Committed in the Territory of Rwanda and Rwandan Citizens Responsible for Genocide and Other such Violations Committed in the Territory of Neighboring States, between January 1, 1994 and December 31, 1994 (1995).
Statute of the International Court of Justice (1945).
South Asian Association for Regional Cooperation on Suppression of Terrorism (1987).
The Hague Conventions of 1899 and 1906.
Treaty on Cooperation among State Members of the Commonwealth of Independent States in Combating Terrorism (1999).
Treaty on the Prohibition of Nuclear Weapons (2017).
Treaty of Peace Between the Allied and Associated Powers and Germany (1918).
United Nations Convention against Transnational Organized Crime (2000), including the Protocol against the Illicit Manufacturing of and Trafficking in Firearms, Their Parts and Components and Ammunition (2001).
United Nations Security Council Resolution 731 (1992).
United Nations Security Council Resolution 748 (1992).
United Nations Security Council Resolution 1044 (1966).
United Nations Security Council Resolution 1054 (1966).
United Nations Security Council Resolution 1267 (1999).
United Nations Security Council Resolution 1333 (2000).
United Nations Security Council Resolution 1368 (2001).
United Nations Security Council Resolution 1373 (2001).

Index

D. Rogers, *Wars, Laws, Rights and the Making of Global Insecurities*, Human Rights Interventions,
https://doi.org/10.1007/978-3-030-90162-2

The manufacturer's authorised representative in the EU is Springer Nature Customer Service Centre GmbH, Europaplatz 3, 69115 Heidelberg, Germany. If you have any concerns regarding our products, please contact ProductSafety@springernature.com

Printed and bound by CPI Group (UK) Ltd, Croydon, CR0 4YY
30/09/2026
02225475-0006